New Rooms for Old Houses

New Rooms for Old Houses

Beautiful Additions for the Traditional Home

Frank Shirley

PHOTOGRAPHS BY RANDY O'ROURKE

The Taunton Press

The Taunton Press
Inspiration for hands-on living®

The Taunton Press, Inc.,
63 South Main Street,
PO Box 5506,
Newtown, CT 06470-5506
e-mail: tp@taunton.com

Editor: Erica Sanders-Foege
Jacket/Cover design: Alison Wilkes
Interior design: Memo Productions Inc., NY
Illustrator: Martha Garstang Hill
Photographer: all photos by Randy O'Rourke, except: pp. 9 (left), 22, 28 (right), 31 (bottom right), 142 (left), 188 (left), 206 (sidebar), 215 (left), 229 (bottom right), 235 (middle & bottom) photos by Frank Shirley Architects; pp. 28 (left, photographer unknown), 193 (bottom left) photos courtesy Frank Shirley Architects; p. 38 (top) photo courtesy Kevin Oreck Architect; pp. 34, 65 (bottom right), 107 (right), 111 (right), 121, 134 (bottom right), 140, 145 (top), 162, 177 (bottom left), 197, 239 photos courtesy the Historic American Building Survey; p. 58 photo courtesy Dover Publications from *American Country Houses of the Gilded Age* by Arnold Lewis, plate #61; p. 134 (top) photo by David S. Gast & Associates; p. 211 photo by Melissa Merrill Floyd; p. 238 (bottom right) photo by Radoslav Opacic Architects; p. 244 (left) photo by Franc Lohsen McCrery Architects

Library of Congress Cataloging-in-Publication Data
Shirley, Frank.
  New rooms for old houses : beautiful additions for the traditional home / Frank Shirley.
     p. cm.
  "National trust book."
  ISBN 978-1-56158-885-5
  1. Dwellings--Remodeling. 2. Buildings--Additions. I. Title.

TH4816.2.S55 2007
690'.837--dc22

                    2007008995

Printed in Singapore
10 9 8 7 6 5 4 3 2 1
The following manufacturers/names appearing in *New Rooms for Old Houses* are trademarks:
Kalwall®, Sherwin-Williams®

The National Trust for Historic Preservation is a private, nonprofit membership organization dedicated to saving historic places and revitalizing America's communities. Recipient of the National Humanities Medal, the Trust was founded in 1949 and provides leadership, education, advocacy, and resources to protect the irreplaceable places that tell America's story. Staff at the Washington, D.C. headquarters, six regional offices and 28 historic sites work with the Trust's 270,000 members and thousands of preservation groups in all 50 states. For more information, visit www.nationaltrust.org.

This book is published under the joint imprint of the National Trust for Historic Preservation and The Taunton Press, Inc.

FOR FRANK AND KATHLEEN, MY MENTORS

Acknowledgments

Imagine one of the caryatids of the Erechtheum. Her poise, stability, and unyielding support I have in my wife, Katherine Gamble. She has read every word of this book many times and provided my most trusted advice. When I was sequestered for long periods writing she filled the void in our family and home, all the while working as a full-time professional and running the books for my office. I admire her strength and am grateful for her help and support.

If having a wonderful wife wasn't enough, I have as a bonus her father, Fred Gamble. Fred has stood by my side from the first sentence, shown me the merits of writing well and was my Occam's razor. His words, advice, and wisdom are inextricably woven into this book.

Much of the experience I share in this book comes from the owners of old houses with whom I've had the privilege of collaborating. Two families have made indelible marks on my practice: Dave and Catie McCool, and Denis and Donna Kokernak are owners who put their trust in me early in my career and inspired me by their vision and dedication to the character of their houses. Many of the ideas in this book took shape as I worked with them.

Contractors make architects look good, and Roger Charron has dressed me in an Armani suit. He has built my finest projects and shown me how to build well. He was always on call for this book.

My editor, Erica Sanders-Foege, made this book possible. I am thankful for her dedication to the book and for her energy, many times swapping emails with me late into the night.

Randy O'Rourke, this book's fine photographer, gave his utmost. He created beautiful photographs that artfully illuminate the book's principles. I enjoyed working with him and am thankful to have his work grace this book.

And finally, I want to thank my children, Olivia and Elias. There is nothing more motivating than a child's embrace. Their hugs energized me even as I left to write over nights and weekends. But now kids, I am done, so let's play!

Contents

You live in an old house and you love it.

You need to add to your old house, but you cherish its original style and want to preserve it. Like you, I prefer old houses— and by old, I mean houses from what I consider the golden era of American residential architecture, 1740 to 1940. For decades, as an architect, I've helped home owners make their old houses more livable. I live in an old house in Cambridge, Massachusetts, with my wife and two young children. Ours is a Victorian house more than 100 years old, and it's almost a member of our family. Should we choose to add onto it, the project would be undertaken with all the deliberation of major surgery on a loved one.

Do you have similar feelings for your home? If so, then keep reading and you will learn how to approach expanding your home, so that the beauty that originally drew you to it is not only preserved but also enhanced. You will discover ways of creating space that you can inhabit more completely, because it will better suit the way you live. For example, your cramped kitchen is expanded, to be the one you dreamed of, large enough for cooking *and* chatting. Whether you already own a historical house or are interested in buying one, you will discover a wealth of ideas and design strategies for creating additions that preserve and build upon the character of your classic home.

ABOVE LEFT: *This lovely Georgian home is historical; built during the golden era but without a critical role in our history.*
ABOVE RIGHT: *This Georgian home was briefly the headquarters for George Washington and later the home of Henry Wadsworth Longfellow. It is considered historic because of its unique place in our nation's history.*

Unless your home is in a legally protected historical district (and most old homes are not), you will be the sole steward of its heritage. I want to help you understand the steps you can take to discharge that responsibility. Should you embrace the task as a privilege, you will be amply rewarded. It's fun, educational, and intriguing. Your reward will be a home of great value and beauty.

HISTORICAL *versus* HISTORIC

A *historical* home is one that was constructed long ago. *Historic* homes were built long ago, too, but they also played a noteworthy role in history. (By the way, it should be noted that the National Trust for Historic Preservation does not make this distinction.) It follows that very few historical homes are also historic. For example, Thomas Jefferson's home, Monticello, and Thomas Edison's home in New Jersey are historic. The houses in *New Rooms for Old Houses* are all historical American homes of the golden era–from 1740 to 1940.

It is important to preserve historic structures as they were at their moment in history. Historic homes require additions that stand off and separate themselves from the house. The National Park Service offers the following guidelines

TOP: *The golden era of architecture witnessed the birth and growth of our nation. The pride we felt is reflected in the homes we built—well crafted and thoughtfully designed, imbued with an enduring beauty.* **BOTTOM:** *Sunlight bathes a new sitting area next to the den and casts golden highlights across the mahogany walls.*

for historic buildings within its jurisdiction: "Additions should be designed and constructed so that the character-defining features of the historic building are not radically changed, obscured, damaged, or destroyed. New design should always be clearly differentiated so that the addition does not appear to be part of the historic resource." This makes sense for historic homes; but for historical homes such as yours and mine, two design ideas are definitely not better than one.

A GUIDING PRINCIPLE:
ACHIEVING HARMONY

For an addition to an old house to work, it must be in harmony with the original structure. If I create an addition for your home and the result is a close marriage of the old and new spaces, the result will be a revitalized residence that remains perfectly composed and blended with its environment. Unfortunately, if I fail, it will be clear even to the untrained eye that something is not right. And, for those with a little bit of know-how, the house will be a puzzling, awkward juxtaposition of alien architectural elements. Picture an old stone farmhouse with a towering two-story addition that features vinyl siding and shutterless windows. Then imagine living in it. You may have the space you need for your new media room and the master suite, but in all likelihood the space will feel disconnected from the rest of the house. Harmony in design not only looks right on the outside but serves and inspires those who inhabit it.

Harmony involves not only appearance, but also function. When I design an addition, I create a floor plan for my clients that considers how the new house will be lived in. I consider the circulation—how people will move about the whole space—and I consider how the rooms are most likely to be used—which ones are major players and which minor? I want my clients to experience their home as one structure: natural, whole, harmonious, and balanced.

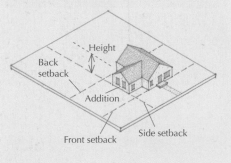

BELOW: *This new formal stair in a Shingle style home is bold and imposing, in accord with the design principles of the style. The materials, white oak and English brown oak, are rich and full of character, reinforcing the design.*

FACING PAGE: *The butler's pantry is small in size but large in function. Linked to the kitchen by its details and materials, it allows cooks easy access to guests enjoying an afternoon tea in the courtyard.*

The living room ceiling of this Spanish Colonial
Revival house is crowned by a dramatic oak truss,
which is stained dark to emphasize its size. Hand-
painted and brightly hued ceramic tiles accent the
large fireplace. Together they give the room an
inviting yet dignified air.

THE FOUR CORNERSTONES

Achieving harmony is not simply a matter of replicating what is already there, but of understanding the design principles of the original home and using them in your addition. To achieve this, there are four fundamental design—I call the four cornerstones—on which all old house expansions should be based: the maintenance of balance, respect for the distinction between public and private areas, the careful use of transitions, and the choice of appropriate materials.

BALANCE   More than any other cornerstone, the balance of design elements determines whether your addition will succeed or fail, be harmonious or stick out as an awkward addendum. Balance is achieved through the proper placement and sizing of your addition. Not surprising, proportion more than anything else governs balance. The proportions of each design element must be correct for the whole design to look right and work well.

The principles of proportion that guided architects building from the golden era—and for most design periods of American residential architecture—are derived from the classical proportions of ancient Greek and Roman architecture. Classical architecture, one of the world's most extraordinary bodies of

ABOVE LEFT: *A fanlight transom, finely shaped casing, and tall windows are assembled symmetrically to present a graceful face toward the public.*
ABOVE RIGHT: *In this Greek Revival room, verticality is emphasized. The window is oversized and its muntins are slimmed to only a half-inch wide.*

thought, mathematically defined the spatial relationships that intuitively feel right to us. For more than two thousand years, these principles have been among the primary means by which beauty has been achieved in architecture and art.

So what brought the golden era to an end? Necessity. Immediately following World War II, an unprecedented demand for new homes was answered by mass-produced housing. As the pursuit of timelessness gave way to the pursuit of timeliness, expediency compromised house design. Consequently, those who love the beauty of classical proportions tend to admire historical homes.

PUBLIC AND PRIVATE AREAS   There was a clear distinction between the public and private areas in an American home built from 1740 to 1940. Public areas were formal. Accordingly, they were located on the first level near the front door for the convenience of guests and precluded easy access to private areas. The living room, dining room, and foyer were formal, and the front facade itself was formal in style. The quality of the finishes in these parts of the house signaled that they were meant for greeting the public.

Private rooms such as bedrooms and kitchens were less formal. Typically, they were located at the rear of the house or on the second floor. At the back of the house you might also find a porch and the service entrance. By their location, their function was easily defined.

ABOUT THE HOUSE Windows Are the Eyes

Windows from historical styles tend to be large and graceful. Proportions, such as the height-to-width ratio of each glass pane and each sash, were carefully determined. Also well managed was the scale of a window's components. Of concern were the muntins, the wood pieces that separate the glass panes. Older windows tend to have thin muntins, about three-quarters of an inch, creating a delicate line in an expanse of glass. Contemporary windows often have wide muntins, which disrupt views.

Also, window-sills of centuries past were thick, sometimes two inches or more, giving the window a solid base on which to sit. Contemporary windowsills are typically three-quarters of an inch and rather

than resting on them, the windows appear to float in the facade. The combination of a more substantial sill and a thinner muntin makes older windows more grounded, and yet more open and graceful. Getting your windows right is among the most important aesthetic considerations of your design.

11

ABOVE: *The rigid symmetry of this grand Federal house left no place for an ell to its side, so it was placed to the rear. It is stepped down in size to express the transition to the informal wing of the house.* **RIGHT:** *Adding and enclosing a porch created a new room for this Gothic Revival.* **FACING PAGE:** *Nooks are private and inviting, such as this secluded spot next to an attic bedroom where the trim and finish are appropriately basic.*

At the front of historical homes you will find the best building materials and the most rigorous execution of design details, such as trim, pilasters, window placement, and entryways. The front of a home may be brick, with elegant pilasters and ornate trim, while the back may be clapboard, with lower eave lines, simpler trim, and looser organization of windows. At the back, the form of the house is more likely to follow the function of the rooms.

An addition that is in harmony with the original structure will reflect this approach to the public and private rooms. Usually, the more formal public rooms of historical houses remain intact and retain their original functions. Because of the growing informality of American culture, most people are interested in additions that increase the informal, private areas of their homes. As a result, additions to historical homes most often belong at the side near the rear or off the rear of the original structure.

Kitchens are a prime example of the growing importance of informal rooms. Historically, kitchens were small, utilitarian spaces where meals were discreetly prepared. Today, home owners prepare meals while visiting with family or guests—

hard to do in the small kitchens of a historical home. It's no surprise that kitchens are frequently the first areas to be expanded. Sometimes they are also opened to an adjoining family room. Because the kitchen and family room are informal, private areas, this openness is very much in accord with the principle of harmony.

Trouble arises, however, when the enthusiasm for openness is carried further and the kitchen is opened to the entry hall. Then a guest coming in the front door is, visually at least, immediately in the kitchen. One may have taken the house into the 21st century, but the spirit, character, and style of the original have been violated. It's like putting on a suit and tie, then pulling out the shirttail.

Many additions involve adding to the side of the original house. When this is done, harmony is maintained if the new facade is in the style of the original. However, care should be taken if an outside entrance is required. Placing it in the front rather than at the side or rear may compromise the formality of the front, and it may mislead guests to enter the home through the family entrance. The front door of a historical home should be treated with great formality. It is intended to be dignified and impressive. When it shares the front facade with an informal entrance, the effect is confusing.

ABOVE: *A deep cased opening, called a portal, separates the two extremes: the kitchen and entrance hall. Historically, a door would have been used, but today many people find such separation unnecessary and inconvenient.* FACING PAGE: *Small rooms can have a big impact. This sunroom with oversized windows gathers abundant sunlight and offers expansive views without injuring the character of the original house.*

ABOVE: *This slender glass wall serves as an effective transition between the disparate forms of a formal house on the right and its informal addition on the left.* RIGHT: *When this Foursquare grew, a cased opening was added to aid the transition from old to new. The opening is broad to make it easy to move between rooms. It is aligned with an original cased opening in the foreground to heighten the procession through the house.*

Garages present another challenge to the maintenance of harmony. Homes that predate the arrival of the automobile were built without a garage, although some had a separate carriage house set off to the rear or side of the house. This arrangement is a rare one these days because convenient, covered access between the house and garage is important.

But adding an attached garage is a challenge given the need to maintain a formal front facade. Avoid adding a broad garage door opening to the front and located in the plane of the front facade. In the metaphor introduced earlier, a garage entrance in the plane of the front facade is like a business suit with tie askew, shirttail out, shoelaces undone, and socks about the ankles—a complete disaster.

TRANSITIONS   Some houses accept an addition with ease. Others are so complete that adding on can quickly and easily take away from their beauty. For example, houses in the Georgian style can be difficult to add to at the sides because they are often buttressed at either end by massive brick and chimney walls. Federals have an elegant simplicity that also can make side additions awkward. Queen Anne Victorians, despite their apparently freewheeling composition, can present the most perplexing challenges. Their shape and compositional organization is complicated, delicately balanced, and three-dimensional, with shapes turning the corners from one side of the house to another. With all four sides of the house working in concert to present a balanced design, finding a place to expand can be difficult, which is why crafting the perfect transition between old and new is crucial.

Transitions between your house and your addition should be of understated design. Inside, their function can vary from a room to an open breezeway. But, in all cases they should avoid introducing new design features, and be sized modestly. Transparency is often effective, as it helps establish the separation between the original building and its addition. A transition should be neutral, quietly continuing some of the subtler design elements of the main house, but always maintaining a subordinate role so that it reads as a connector and not a third destination.

When the functions of the rooms where the house and addition meet are incompatible transitions are also useful. One common example is a new garage next to a kitchen. You won't be happy when the cold air and fumes of the garage invade the space you use for preparing meals. An intervening space between them is the answer. I often add a mudroom—a transition that helps soften these juxtapositions, easing the harshness of conflicting styles or functions.

Transitions take on a different meaning when used to discuss the connecting of inside to outside. A common contemporary addition is the creation of livable

THE ART OF CRAFT   **The Hat on a House**

Your roof is like the hat on your head; if there is something wrong with your hat, no one will fail to see it. Rooflines are an integral part of a historical home's design. Sometimes the roof shape is the most distinctive feature, such as the mansard roof of a Second Empire home. When planning your addition, carefully consider the resulting roofline.

Old vs. New Windows

Clients often ask me to replace their old windows, but it is an unnecessary expense. It's not that the windows have run out of useful life; rather, they are perceived to be an energy sieve. A recent study showed that the R-value (a measure of how easily heat flows through a material) of a typical old wooden window—one sheet of glass with a storm panel—is nearly identical to that of a thermal-pane window—two sheets of glass sandwiching inert gas.

Old windows are solidly constructed of old growth woods and have an unlimited life if you paint them every 10 years and replace the glazing putty every 50 years. Replacement windows of new growth wood are much less durable. So keep those old windows and use storm panels. With a little care, they will last for decades to come and be just as energy efficient.

space outdoors, such as covered and screened porches and terraces. Common tools to aid in the transition between interior and exterior, these elements bring nature into the house. A screened porch allows you to move outside to enjoy breezes and views while still enjoying some of the benefits of the interior, such as protection from insects and the sun. A covered porch provides cover from rain while you are holding your groceries and fumbling for your keys. A porch can also be an outdoor room where a neighbor can stop by, sit, and chat without you worrying about the mess inside. Raised terraces blur the line between interior and exterior, especially if floor materials are shared between the room and adjacent terrace.

MATERIALS   Materials express your home's personality. A brick home feels different from a wooden home and a clapboard home feels different from a shingle home, no matter the design style. Materials can also call forth romantic recollections, such as the stucco walls of the New Orleans' French Colonials and the red tile roofs of California's Spanish Revivals. In these examples the material captures the architectural spirit of the emigrants' homeland.

Materials also reinforce the distinction between formal and informal. The finest materials were traditionally reserved for the front of the house, while more economical materials were used on the side and rear elevations and in

ABOVE: *Without knowing the use of either building or having a glimpse of its entry, we can discern that the red building is the more formal structure here. Clapboards are more refined in appearance than the vertical flush boards of the yellow building.*

FACING PAGE: *This new bay window is well-balanced. The windows are tall, and fill the bay with an expanse of glass. Muntins are thin and delicate to maximize views. And trim carefully follows classical proportions appropriate for this French Colonial Revival home.*

private rooms. Brick front facades may give way to clapboard at the side and rear, and clapboard front facades may give way to shingles. Materials of construction in historical homes also varied regionally, because long-distance transportation was costly and the demands of climate and culture differed.

Materials used on historical homes were harvested or mined from the earth: wood, stone, brick, slate, and various metals. I try to work with these when adding to historical homes. Their warmth, solidity, texture, and tactile qualities are familiar, inviting, and comforting. Such materials are without peers. While most are still available, the costs of some have risen so much that synthetic alternatives are often chosen. But the success of these varies dramatically.

As with the other design considerations, harmony is achieved when the materials for your addition are selected with an understanding of the original choice of materials. As in so many areas of our concern, simply copying from the original structure has its pitfalls.

A BEAUTIFUL ADDITION

Now you have the fundamental idea: a beautiful addition is yours when you achieve harmony, and the achievement of harmony rests upon the four design cornerstones I previously outlined. In the following chapters, I'll apply these concepts to additions on houses of many design periods. If I succeed in my efforts, you will finish this book with a large collection of design tools that you can use to think and speak clearly and effectively about your own dreams for a new room on your old house.

PRECEDING SPREAD: *There is no substitute for materials mined from the earth. Old houses are made of natural materials, and no two stones, bricks, or clay tiles are exactly the same. Used on a wall, roof, or floor, natural materials form a visual symphony.* **FACING PAGE:** *At the end of the day, when harmony is achieved between new and old you will have ample cause to pull out a chair and enjoy the beauty of your efforts.*

TRAIN WRECK Raze the Roof

This Colonial Revival house once was dignified. High symmetry, bay windows, a large arched entry, and a bold, classically influenced cornice coalesced into a handsome facade. Unfortunately, someone enlarged this house with no appreciation for its quality. Where the strong edge of the cornice met the sky, now lies an irregular box that has nothing in common with its host. It even fails to respect the historical house's footprint. Unless a Good Samaritan comes along and removes this transgression, this old house will be forever blemished.

1

PRESERVING
THE BALANCE
OF YOUR HOME

*"If I were asked to say what is at once
the most important production of Art and
the thing most to be longed for,
I should answer, a beautiful House."*
–William Morris

What is balance? You might answer, "I know it when I see it," and you would probably be right. But consider that things you admire—whether they are homes, paintings, or flower arrangements—are intentionally balanced. Somebody composed them to be so. Adding randomly to such a composition could easily upset the balance and take away from the beauty of the work. By balance, I mean a visual balance that is simply an extension of what we experience as physical balance. A seesaw is balanced when children of the same weight sit on opposite sides equidistant from the center. A seesaw is also balanced when a heavier child is near the center and a lighter child is farther from the center on the opposite side, in an asymmetrical arrangement.

TOP LEFT: *This home was a symmetrical Georgian, two stories tall. But a taller addition has been added to the back and side, dominating the original house. The chimney in the foreground once marked the roof's ridge and the house's center, but no longer. With the third floor addition in the back, the only remnant of the old saltbox roofline is a piece of trim.*

TOP RIGHT: *The character of this historical home is preserved despite an addition that nearly doubled its size. The addition, on the right, is scaled down from the original house and also placed to the side and rear, leaving the public facade intact. Its materials are the same, but its details are simplified.*

When you're talking about adding on to an old house, balance is an essential cornerstone in maintaining the harmony of the whole structure. You can't add on randomly or you'll have a train wreck when you're finished. When designing an addition for a period-style house, counterbalancing one volume, by which I mean a distinct three-dimensional shape with another creates visual stability. Of course, we are also taking into consideration other visual elements like size, color, shadow, form, pattern, texture, and material. For example, a black shape appears heavier than a white one of the same size. And, as in the seesaw example, symmetrical and asymmetrical visual balance work equally well.

Take, for example, two Colonial era homes (see the photos above). They have several things in common: both were built in the early 19th century, their front facades are a repeating rhythm of windows, their entries mark the center, and both have undergone a significant expansion. But there is one important difference between these homes: Since their additions, one house lost its balance while the other maintained it.

If you can see the difference, then you accomplish balance when you see it. The question then becomes, how do you know balance before you see it, so that after you build an addition your home resembles the one on the right and not the one on the left? If you can't answer this easily, you

This addition is in harmony with the original Federal style house. It is smaller and placed to the rear, preserving the old house's character. And its materials and proportions are sympathetic to the style.

The Golden Mean

The Greeks discovered the most famous ratio, the Golden Mean, also known as the Golden Section or Phi (ϕ). It cannot be expressed with a finite number of digits, but is approximately 1.618. Phi has many remarkable mathematical and geometric properties. For example, from a Golden Rectangle (length to width ratio equal to Phi) you can subtract a square whose sides equal the rectangle's width, leaving a smaller rectangle that is also golden. If you continue this indefinitely, the resulting squares form the scaffolding for a spiral found throughout nature, for example, in seashells, pinecones, flowers, and pineapples. Phi was used in the design of many highly esteemed buildings including the Parthenon and Notre Dame Cathedral in Paris.

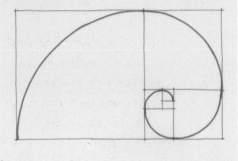

are not alone. People have been pondering the question for millennia. Fortunately, our ancestors have discovered some answers for us.

WHY BALANCE MATTERS

Lopsided, cockeyed, top-heavy, or unstable—these are ways we describe something that we see as visually unbalanced. (So far no client has come to me wanting a house designed along these lines.) When we see something that is unbalanced, we feel anxious, either consciously or otherwise. We yearn for visual balance, either consciously or unconsciously, and when it exists, we experience a feeling of stability and well-being.

As a society, we have sought to bring order to our environment, to organize our surroundings, to create a balanced world. Before us, the Greeks began to apply mathematical relationships to building design, believing that the abstract mathematical relationships they had discovered governed the natural world and aesthetics. They elevated and refined the pursuit of balance in architecture.

We see this in nature—the beautiful structures of seashells, snowflakes, and pinecones all follow mathematical rules. So, we seek balance, in part, because it is natural. Unstable structures are not part of nature, at least not for long.

Consider the two Colonial era homes I mentioned on page 28. Your attention is probably held for no more than a glance by the unbalanced home because the house is a collage of awkwardly joined parts that are as visually engaging as an unassembled puzzle. Probably the second house stops you in your tracks as it does me, and you continue gazing to admire it. If the first house is a collection of puzzle pieces, the second is a puzzle tightly assembled to present a beautiful picture. Each part of the house takes its cues from the rest of the house. This unifies the house and gives it an air of repose and refinement. The house is aesthetically pleasing. These attributes of a well-balanced home are important to the eye, the mind, and the spirit. This is why balance matters.

BALANCING OLD WITH NEW Balance takes on critical proportions when talking about expanding an old house. Take, for example, the folk Italianate home with an addition (see the bottom right photo above). The original house is a mid-nineteenth-century structure. The addition fails to relate to it. Instead, it sports its own identity. As a result, the home appears as two random structures that suffered the misfortune of being attached. The timelessness of the original home is shattered.

When you plan an addition to your home, balance can only be achieved if the addition looks like a natural extension of the original work. Otherwise, the new part of your home will scream, "Look at me! I'm the addition!"

FACING PAGE: *A new room can have a life all its own while carrying forward the ideas of the original house. Here a new sunroom is enclosed with glass, whose pane size matches that of the original double-hung windows. The muntins, too, are a match. Supporting the windows is a wall finished traditionally with vertical, wooden boards and a simple base.*
LEFT: *Wood paneled walls, leaded glass windows, and Art Nouveau lighting are all defining forms that mark this house as British Arts and Crafts.* **BELOW:** *We strive for balance and out of it find beauty, such as in this symmetrical arrangement of flower pots.*

ACHIEVING BALANCE

How can we achieve balance? As amusing as it may seem, this question comes up each year in my home as we decorate our Christmas tree. Our children are too young to participate, so we have two decorators, my wife and me. We each have our own ideas about the project. Over the years, we have learned that to avoid butting heads we must work on opposite sides of the tree. However, to achieve balance we must switch sides frequently so that we preserve the natural balance of the symmetrical tree. By blending our ideas we have created our own style. Applying it uniformly gives us a beautiful, symmetrically balanced tree that appears as the creation of one mind. Of course, you will not

be designing your home this way, but you will be facing challenges uniquely your own and you can have fun dealing with them creatively.

So that you can have more enjoyment than frustration designing your addition let's look at three tools to assist you with the challenge. I call these tools *defining forms, precedents,* and *design rules.*

IDENTIFYING THE MAIN FEATURES   *What are the defining forms?* I start with this question as it helps me get to know the house. I look to identify dominant features. For example, I consider the roof, the windows, the trim, and the walls. I look for features that are common, repeating themselves throughout (dentils, exposed rafter tails, the number of lights in a sash), as well as features that are unique (a Palladian window, a conical roof at a corner, swags around a covered entry). In each style you find that certain building elements have come to stand for that style, such as the steeply pitched gable roof of a Gothic Revival or the dark half-timbered facade of a Tudor.

THE ART OF CRAFT

The Orders of Greek Architecture

Doric, Ionic, and Corinthian are the three styles, or orders, of Greek temple architecture, all of which are based on columns supporting beams called entablatures. The columns have three elements: a base, a shaft, and a capital. So does the entablature: an architrave, a frieze, and a cornice. Within each order, the proportional dimensions of each element are specified so that given the diameter of the column, the dimensions and placement of all elements could be calculated. Adopted by the Romans, we have been using it ever since.

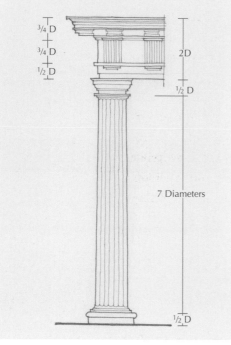

Take note of the defining features of your home; they are the key words, or vocabulary, in the language of the house. Just as you wouldn't arbitrarily use an Italian word in a Russian text because you like the sound of that word, you shouldn't drop architectural features of a foreign language into the design of your addition. For example, the mansard roof that caps Second Empire homes should not cap the addition to your Bungalow. This may be an obvious example. But neither should Georgian dentils parade along a Federal facade nor should classical columns support Gothic Revival porches. All are examples of mixing vocabularies into architectural gibberish.

STUDYING PRECEDENTS   *What are the precedents for adding to a house of your home's style?* When I am faced with a challenging house, particularly one that seems to defy expansion, I look for examples of how others added to houses of a similar style both in new construction and in historical examples. In recently constructed additions, I may find solutions to practical requirements similar to my own, such as needing a new home office or family room. Suppose I need to design an attached garage for an Italianate home. If I look around the neighborhood and find an Italianate with a recently added garage, I'm in luck. Where did they place the garage? Which way do the doors face? How is the addition unified with the house?

Examples of homes with historical additions are also valuable to me, because I can learn how a style was expanded early in its life. The builder who added to the Italianate not long after it was constructed would likely be well versed in that style, given that he was building the addition when the style was popular. How the builder chose to expand the house gives me a peek into the minds of Italianate builders. I can discern their perception of balance, as well as see how they preserved balance when altering the original house.

THE RULES OF DESIGN

What are the design rules? The architectural forms and elements, from windows to roofs, are your vocabulary. The design rules are your grammar. Together they are the design language of your home. Think of Goldilocks and her search for things "just right." This is our goal, too. We want changes to our cherished old house to be just right. A key difference, of course, is that we do not have the option of choosing between additions. We have to get it right the first time. How? There are three key design rules that have been studied and used for millennia: proportion, regulating lines, and symmetry.

These design rules are guidelines for adding or changing the building elements that define your home. They help bring order to your design and winnow the possibilities by revealing that certain design solutions are more appropriate than others. For example, chances are you'll be adding windows in your addition. The rules help you determine what size they might be and how many panes they

FACING PAGE: *This 1833 Greek Revival was added to in 1846 while the style was still popular. The addition is defined by the same classical formality of the house, but its details have been scaled down: the cornice and windows are smaller, the roof is lower, and no porch was added.*
LEFT: *The new garage (to the right) is linked to the mudroom with a breezeway. As a recently constructed addition, it shows the successful relationship between the house and yard.*

will hold—all based on the style of your home. Or they can help you determine how high your new kitchen ceiling should be or how long your new living room should be. In this way the design rules help you carefully assemble your new space, from its overall shape to the size of the trim in a room.

Each rule has a specific task. Proportions guide an architectural form's apparent size. Regulating lines bring organization to facades and rooms. They align elements and create patterns. Symmetrical and asymmetrical balance work to ensure that the house and addition coalesce into a pleasing home.

PROPORTION Proportion is the quantitative relationship between two parts, the ratio. When you make salad dressing, the proportion of oil to vinegar is critical—too much oil and your dressing is greasy and bland. Too much vinegar and your salad is too tart to eat. Architectural examples of important ratios are the width of a window to its height and the length of a room to its width. When we like the feel of a room this may well be because of the ratio of its length to its width. In such cases you might say the room is "well-proportioned." The essence of a ratio's success lies in its ability to distinguish between the viable and the absurd. Proper ratios, or proportions, steer you away from a house more appropriate for Alice in her wonderland journey and toward a house that anyone would want to visit.

What makes certain ratios work? Perhaps it involves the ratio's connection to nature. Perhaps ratios unify the smallest parts with the largest, like a grand unification theory scientists seek for our universe. But, no matter the cause,

FACING PAGE: The addition to the rear of this Queen Anne follows the rules of design and joins the old house in a satisfying way. It is proportioned to appear smaller than the historical house and its forms are asymmetrically arranged, in step with the original. ABOVE: *The front entry of this French Colonial home follows the proportions of the Renaissance, which defines the relationship of height to width for the columns, capitals, and entablature. Renaissance architects, such as Andrea Palladio, followed the proportional systems of classical Rome.*

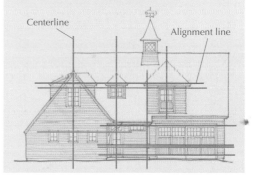

I have found in my projects that certain ratios, like the golden section or the harmonic proportions, generate rooms and facades that satisfy. Such homes are visually balanced; they make us feel comfortable.

REGULATING LINES   Regulating lines are imaginary lines that designers use to position building elements such as doors and windows on the facade. Their primary role is to organize the many elements that make a house, similar to a grid organizing the layout of a city. Regulating lines are almost always used on the layout of facades, but are frequently used in floor plans, too. In a floor plan, regulating lines may be used to center a door in a room, or to frame a view through a window at the end of a hall; on a facade, regulating lines may be used to align the tops of windows. Regulating lines sometimes run across the

TOP: *No regulating lines were used on this facade, giving it a dysmorphic appearance.* LEFT: *The porch of this Gothic Revival is proportioned to be tall and slender, highlighted by the gravity-defying columns. The designer wanted it to soar like the medieval cathedrals that were the inspiration.* FACING PAGE: *Regulating lines sometimes become a design element, such as the picture rail in this image that wraps the original dining and living rooms. As a regulating line, it sets the height of the cased openings and windows; as a picture rail, it allows artwork to be hung without nails.*

facade at an angle reflective of the proportioning system. Their purpose is always to help establish a pleasing order among the building elements.

SYMMETRY AND ASYMMETRY   Just as a boat is designed to be stable in water, so too should your house be stable on ground. A stable house is a balanced house. Symmetry and asymmetry are the rules by which your home's balance is achieved. Symmetry is achieved when two halves of a facade mirror each other. Symmetrical facades have a restful balance. The two halves of an asymmetrical facade are different from each other, but their visual weights about the center are equal. Asymmetrical facades have a dynamic balance. One side is not a mirror image of the other, but balance is achieved by creating the same visual weight on

A Study in Contrasts

Thomas Jefferson's Virginia home, Monticello, and the Gamble House in California, the Arts and Crafts gem designed by architects Greene and Greene, are exquisite designs that show us contrast in achieving balance: Monticello through symmetry, the Gamble House through asymmetry.

Monticello (below, top) draws on the ideals of the Renaissance, which emphasized strict order and classical forms. If you draw a centerline through the entry of Monticello, every shape, window, and building material to the left is identical to and a mirror image of that on the right. Symmetrical houses are inherently balanced. They can look solid, calm, and elegant.

The Gamble House (below, bottom) is an example of asymmetrical balance—it's not inherent, but must be artfully composed.

Dividing the facade in half yields a left side and a right side that are different from each other. The large gable that steps forward just left of the centerline dominates. To the right a horizontal wing extends to a bi-level porch. The wing, in combination with a third floor that is shifted to the right of the centerline, brings the facade into balance. Asymmetrical houses feel vibrant and at times edgy.

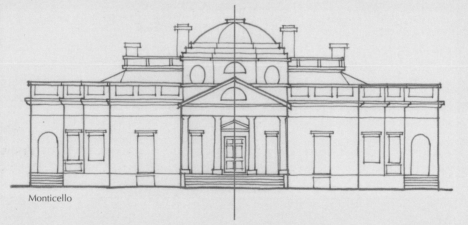

Monticello

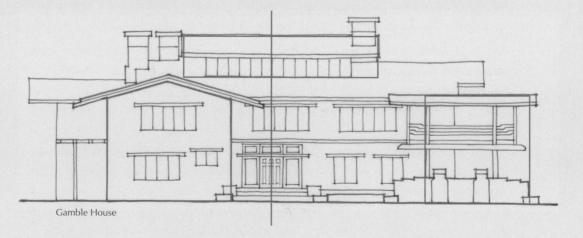

Gamble House

Frank Lloyd Wright's masterpiece, Fallingwater, is a magnificent display of asymmetrical balance. Porches and roofs jut out in different directions, but are balanced about the central stone wall.

each side. Some styles, like Georgian, are defined by symmetry, while styles such as Queen Anne are invariably asymmetrical—take care to note which is used in your home.

PUTTING IT ALL TOGETHER

Think of George Washington's home, Mt. Vernon. Its columns are comfortably proportioned. They appear solid but not squat, tall but not spindly. Its windows are well-proportioned; they are large, drawing appropriate attention to their important role as givers of light. At the same time, they are intimate, even delicate, because of the small panes within the window. Casing widths are chosen in proportion to the windows they surround, just as a frame is carefully sized for a prized painting. If you look closely, you can see how the tops of windows and doors align horizontally. The roof is nicely sized for the house it covers, capping it as a capital completes a column. Each part of the house takes its cues from the rest of the house. This unifies the house, and this is why it stands in your mind as a symbol of classic architecture. By choosing window, door, and roof shapes that are proportionally and stylistically related, the final result is a well-composed facade. You are now using a design language.

ABOUT THE HOUSE

An Air-Conditioned Old House

Integrating a contemporary convenience, like air-conditioning, into the ambiance of an old room requires cunning. Air-conditioning cools the room via a supply duct and recycles it back through a return duct. A supply duct is small, usually no longer than twelve inches, and placed in every room. Manufacturers have many handsome grilles of various patterns and materials to cover supplies.

Returns are a different matter. Only a few are placed throughout the house, usually toward the center, and each is quite large—about 20 in. by 24 in.—which can disrupt a room's harmony. Work with your mechanical contractor to locate each return grille in an inconspicuous location, or place it so that the grille becomes a part of the room's design.

When contemplating the design of your addition, first learn the design language of your home, then apply it to the addition. The continuity of language between old and new will unify your home and maintain its spirit.

Achieving balance between old and new, while preserving the balance of the old should be the foremost goal when designing your addition. By learning the language of your old home and studying what has come before, you will have the tools with which to design an addition. And you will not be compromising the balance and spirit of the older structure. With care, you may enhance them.

FACING PAGE: *New or old? An addition well-balanced with its predecessor will continue a legacy of timelessness.* **LEFT:** *Arches in a line frame the way to the master bedroom. Plaster corners, inset door frames, and dark bronze hardware define the style of this Spanish Colonial. Antique Moroccan lanterns recall the origins of the style*

A HOME ON THE HUDSON

French Colonial · Irvington, New York

The owners of this 1927 French Country home knew balance when they saw it–it was love at first sight. The house fit them perfectly, but with the arrival of each new grandchild, the fit got tighter and tighter. With careful consideration, and with grandparents' hearts, they decided to enlarge their home. The owners wanted a new kids' bedroom with a play area, a family room for everyone to gather, and a larger kitchen to feed them all.

When I first visited the home, I was impressed by its quiet radiance. The house was unassuming–the front door stood barely a step above the ground–and yet unshakably graceful. It was the Audrey Hepburn of houses. Originally, the building was home to the staff of an estate on the Hudson River. A structure much smaller than the estate house, it still reflected elegant proportions. The home found its architectural roots in the countryside Renaissance homes of France and Italy, which feature tall, narrow doors and windows, and detailing with classical proportions.

Originally a seasonal porch, the light-filled sunroom was rebuilt to make it weather tight and, with radiant heat under the tile, warm in the cold months. The owners, accomplished gardeners, enjoy expansive views of their grounds in the summer, and cultivate their indoor plants during the winter.

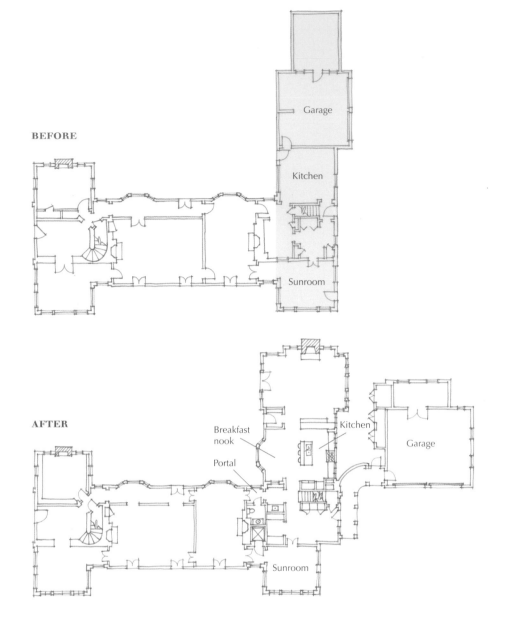

BEFORE

Garage

Kitchen

Sunroom

AFTER

Breakfast
nook

Portal

Kitchen

Garage

Sunroom

TOP: *Before the addition, a stubby garage wing to the left sat on the back side of the house.* RIGHT: *The new rooms are organized along an axis that defines circulation. A portal separates the formal and informal rooms of the house. Bay windows and French doors open up views and provide access to the yard.* FACING PAGE: *The French doors open the family room onto the private courtyard. The doors have narrow stiles and rails that accentuate their slender proportion. Muntins align and unify the doors, sidelights, and transoms.* FOLLOWING SPREAD: *The addition, to the left, defines a new outdoor room: the courtyard. A lower eave line sets the addition off from the main house while pop-up dormers and a butler's pantry door break down its symmetry and mark its informal use. A slate roof and stucco facade match the original house and link old with new.*

CREATING A COURTYARD

How do you expand such a home? It is shaped like an "I," with the formal entry at the bottom. Architect Radoslav Opacic placed the addition out of public view, creating an ell-shaped plan and preserving the original scale. This created a private courtyard onto which new and old rooms open.

Opacic's decision to drop the new eave line 16 in. below the original proved critical to the project's success. Because its roof is lower, the addition defers to the house. At the end of the addition is a turned gable, which provides needed headroom and acts as a "stop" to the elevation, like a period at the end of sentence. Defining elements from the original house, such as the bay window, carry over to the addition. Together these design features create a well-composed facade in the spirit of the original.

ROOMS DESIGNED
FOR COMFORT

The new kitchen and family room are open to each other making it easy for kids and grownups to socialize. A peninsula between the rooms defines each while preserving the openness. Both rooms are designed to be no bigger than needed: The kitchen has one wall of counter and cabinets, modest for many homes today. However, the large island draws your attention and creates the illusion of a larger kitchen.

The family room is snug. Anchored by a fireplace with a French limestone mantel, the family room beckons all to come relax. For both rooms the ceiling was raised higher than elsewhere in the house so that ceiling heights are in proportion to room size.

A new bedroom for the grandkids is the focus upstairs. The height of this room is diminished from above and below; the raised ceiling of the family room lifts the floor, while the addition's lower roof drops the ceiling. Out of this predicament came opportunity. Opacic designed a tray ceiling and carried it around all four sides so that the walls are scaled for young guests. A picture rail wraps the room marking the top of the wall. Windows lower than usual are a kid-friendly gesture. Cubbies are carved out under the tray ceiling into which beds, dressers, and a play area are tucked. Together these create a room proportioned for children.

ABOVE: *Grandkids can steal away to different cubbies that wrap the room. Shorter walls and lower windows make the room charming and inviting.*
FACING PAGE: *An easy flow defines the relationship between the kitchen and family room. Terra-cotta tile floor and salvaged oak beams link the rooms. Salvaged oak flooring, sealed with polyurethane, caps the counters and unifies the room's palette.*

ATTENTION TO DETAIL

The windows, which the owners were passionate about, embodied the graceful elegance of the home, so the new windows had to be just right. They chose to have them custom made so they would match the proportions of the originals down to the muntins, and have energy-saving thermal panes.

In fact, the whole addition's success lies in its sensitive attention to proportion: from its placement to its shape, down to the dimensions of the window details.

SAVING BEAUTY

Shingle Style · Coastal Massachusetts

Overlooking the Atlantic Ocean atop a 60-ft. granite cliff, this 1883 Shingle style home had lost its balance. Once bold and elegant, it sat exposed and tired; storms, time, and poor renovations had taken their toll. Originally, the house featured a tower, that dominated the front facade, provided a focal point, and visually anchored the house to its granite foundation. But 50 years ago, a winter storm toppled that tower and the subsequent renovation paid little heed to the home's character, leaving it with a meek appearance. The original design also featured a prominent porte cochere that announced the home's entry. Later, the porte cochere was replaced with an incongruous colonial entry.

On the inside, the front entry was small and dark, too small for a house of such stature. It was painfully constrained by a cumbersome, ill-lit staircase, which had been accommodated by dropping the entryway ceiling to 7 ft. The new owners wanted a more inviting entry, in scale with their home.

An addition to the front of this house returned it to grandeur. Extending 6 ft. beyond the original facade, the addition (at left in the photo) is capped by a broad gable roof. Windows are arranged asymmetrically for a bold appearance.

ABOVE: *Without its defining features, the facade falls flat. A few bad renovations later, it had been twice replicated but still couldn't fill the shoes of the original tower (top right). The ill-conceived Colonial frontispiece addition didn't help.* ABOVE RIGHT: *This photo, taken not long after the house was built, shows the dominant tower in the foreground with the porte cochere behind.* FACING PAGE: *This cozy seat is a relaxing haven in the entry hall, and recalls nineteenth century living halls that were designed as a place to both greet and relax.*

BRINGING BACK THE STYLE

The house was clearly out of balance, but the owners, recognizing that the bones of the structure were sound, committed to an expansion. They recounted to me numerous weekend drives studying precedents, taking photographs of Shingle style homes, and sometimes stopping to measure key elements. They considered—and rejected—the idea of rebuilding the tower. This would neither improve the dark and uninviting entry, nor add space where needed.

The owners decided that an addition in the spirit of the original was the best approach. To restore balance inside and out, the middle third of the front facade was extended 6 ft. and capped with a large cross-gable roof. This simple change had a profound effect.

A SPACIOUS ENTRY HALL

The addition provided much needed space to the foyer and stair and allowed for two simple but dramatic changes. First, the direction of the stair was reversed so that as it descended it flowed into the foyer, greeting visitors with a charismatic welcome. Second, the addition was left open to the second floor, creating a soaring space through which all house activities now pass.

The previously forbidding entry is now an inviting room. Its scale is in proportion to the scale of the house; both the entry and the house have a strong, dramatic presence appropriate for the spectacular site they inhabit. The weight of the tall, rectangular door is asymmetrically balanced with the broad, curved stair. Balance

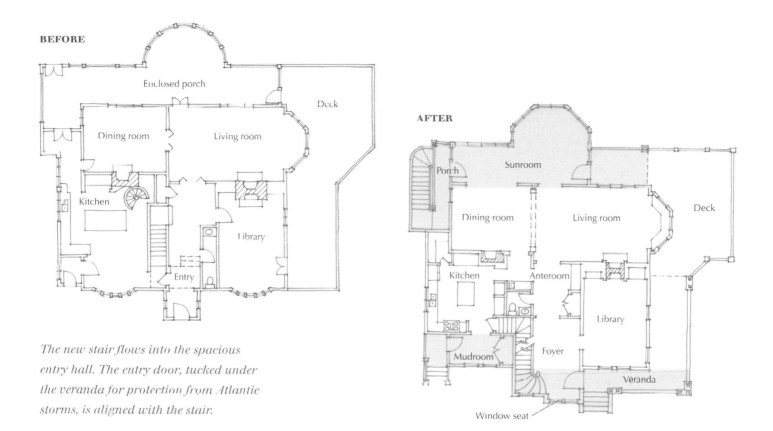

Enclosed porch

Deck

Dining room

Living room

Kitchen

Library

Entry

Porch

Sunroom

Dining room

Living room

Deck

Kitchen

Anteroom

Library

Mudroom

Foyer

Veranda

Window seat

The new stair flows into the spacious
entry hall. The entry door, tucked under
the veranda for protection from Atlantic
storms, is aligned with the stair.

can be found in the details, too. A crown molding over 15 in. tall caps the two-story
room. The crown molding found elsewhere in the house none of which exceed
5 in.–would have been too small for the entry. It would have been out of balance.

Regulating lines organize the defining elements of the stair hall. Large windows are stacked three high and aligned with the stair, providing a continuous
exterior view when descending the stairs. The stairs, in turn, end opposite the
entry door. Cased openings are aligned front to back defining circulation without a
confining corridor. The window seat, aligned with the cased openings, gives guests
approaching on the outside walk a view through the house to the ocean beyond.

A REVITALIZED FACADE

Since the removal of the porte cochere and the storm's damage to the tower, the facade had lost its defining elements.
The addition is capped by a new defining element: an imposing gable roof. The gable extends to the house's edge, and is
the first thing you see when you look at the facade. Whereas
the tower acted as the focal point for the original house, the
gable now takes center stage, and several individual elements

FACING PAGE: *From the entry hall, views*
of the water beckon one to proceed to the
vista-filled rooms beyond. An axis, or
regulating line, organizes the rooms and
windows to frame the water view and
heighten the anticipation.

The Shingle Style

It is not the wood shingle itself, but how the wood shingle is used that is unique to the Shingle style. Architects exploring the Shingle style were emboldened by the less formal designs of their Queen Anne predecessors. H. H. Richardson and McKim, Mead, and White, et al., weary of the use of ornament in earlier Victorian homes, sought a more relaxed, cottage-like aesthetic. This pursuit, coupled with a fresh look at the materials and shapes of buildings from medieval France and England, led to the Shingle style.

The wood shingle was essential in expressing the fluidity and elasticity of the house's exterior. By using only one material, Shingle architects accentuated the dynamic and asymmetrical shapes and forms of their designs. Towers, bows and bays, dramatic roof lines, and deeply recessed windows soon became associated with the style. Covered in shingles and unencumbered by other ornamental details, the sophisticated compositions at the heart of the style are accentuated. The humble wood shingle was reinvented as a graceful, even sensual, design tool, and a truly American style flourished.

coalesce around it. As the massive trunk of a tree balances its freeform branches, the large gable balances the deep soffit, shingled bracket, and curved walls. Without the gable they would be visual oddities.

The home owners worked within the language, or the historical design elements, of the original house by repeating the steeply-pitched gable roof. The new gable roof also relates to the existing diminutive dormer to its left and accentuates a major-minor relationship. The new gable says, "Look at me." Such a gesture is more than surface deep, for under its broad span lies the centerpiece of the home: the new entry and stair hall.

The addition exploits the Shingle style language with an asymmetrical arrangement of shapes and forms, carefully organized to present a dynamic balance. Trim is used minimally in favor of a skin of shingles that wraps the building uninterrupted. To express the elasticity of the shingle skin, the walls are curved in and out and the shingles follow. Even the large bracket supporting the new gable roof is sheathed in shingles.

Today this home is an imposing structure resting confidently in an awesome setting. It says, "I'm going to be here, powerful and beautiful and enchanting, for a very long time."

The house's bold perch is evident from the beach below. The new turned gable, so distinct on the front facade, has a quieter presence on the side.

BALANCING INSIDE AND OUT

Spanish Colonial Revival · Los Angeles, California

When the owner bought this 1926 Spanish Colonial Revival in Los Angeles, it was 1,800 sq. ft. with two bedrooms. All other bidders had planned to raze it and build mansions. But where they had seen a vacant lot, the then-prospective owner saw a jewel: a graceful home, warm and inviting, with handcrafted tiles, custom cabinetry, and well-proportioned rooms. To enjoy southern California's equable climate, she envisioned an outdoor dining area. And, by adding a master suite, a family room, and a larger kitchen, the home would accommodate her needs with ease.

For architect Kevin Oreck, the greatest challenge would be to add more than 1,100 sq. ft. of space while preserving the home's human scale. He did not want to alter the home's lovely but modest face, so he looked to the rear of the house to expand. There he found a bland, attached garage, a liability that became an asset when he expanded the footprint of the garage and converted it to a family room—light-filled, airy, and spacious with French doors that open to a private yard.

Today, the renovated and expanded kitchen opens to a dining patio with a fireplace and grille. Inside, the kitchen and family room ceilings are raised to make their height proportional to the room size. A new, detached garage in the back corner of the yard provides a pleasant landscaping backdrop.

New and old frame the inviting dining patio. New French doors lead from the kitchen and closely match the originals beyond. Because building codes required doors wider than the original ones, the architect adjusted the width and height to maintain their proportion.

ABOVE: *The low-pitched roof, restful sym-*
metry, and restrained vocabulary make
the original front facade warm and invit-
ing. Tucked behind, the addition is barely
perceptible. A corner of its roof can be
seen behind the living room roof. RIGHT:
A master bedroom reigns supreme on
the second floor, enjoying materials and
finishes other bedrooms do not. For a
connection to the outdoors, the bedroom
addition is to the rear and opens onto the
backyard through an expanse of French
doors out of public view.

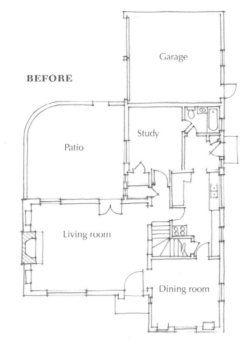

BEFORE

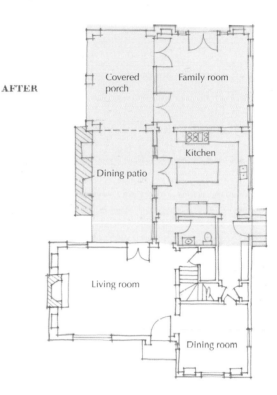

AFTER

The outdoor rooms, comfortable and intimate, are framed by the addition's walls.

A MASTERFUL SUITE UPSTAIRS

Upstairs, what was the desolate roofscape of the garage is now a cheerful master bedroom. This showpiece of the second floor has a cathedral ceiling like that of the original living room. Exposed oak trusses spanning the width are appropriately simplified from those of the more formal living room. A viewing deck overlooking the backyard opens the room to the outdoors. Clever placement of the bath and walk-in closet extends the master bedroom beyond the first floor and creates a covered porch below, offering a welcome respite from the noon sun.

By converting the old garage space for most of the first floor addition, the unassuming scale of the original house is preserved despite the significant expansion of living area. The second floor addition follows the original house's straightforward shape and the simple symmetry of the facade. Viewed from the backyard, the addition blends quietly with the house beyond. From the front it is nearly invisible. The addition is taller, but it is set back nearly 25 ft. from the front facade and the roof pitch is identical, keeping it out of view.

A COMMON VOCABULARY

Oreck, like the owner, appreciated the distinctive design elements and handcrafted materials of the house. Rather than introducing a new lexicon, he used the house's original vocabulary. Inside, he repeated key touches such as arched openings, decorative ceramic tiles, and oak beams and floors, linking the new to the old. The plaster finish on the new walls was hand-troweled to leave pockmark imperfections, matching the "Santa Barbara" finish of the older structures. Outside, the original vocabulary was simple: whitewashed stucco walls, low pitched red Spanish tile roofs, and turquoise-colored doors and windows. The addition followed suit.

Details stand out in a home of such restrained vocabulary, and Oreck was attentive to the details. For example, the decorative, glazed tiles are flush with the plaster, a handcrafted and time-consuming detail that harks back to an earlier time.

All the door and window hardware that was removed during the renovation was salvaged and reused. It would have been quicker, easier, and perhaps cheaper to discard it, but a part of the house's character would have gone with it. Where

TOP: A sense of balance emanates from this original dining room niche and cabinet. It is just the right size for the room and serves as a guide for much of the new cabinetry. **FACING PAGE:** *An arched opening connects the new kitchen with the family room and garden. Simple light cabinetry makes for a nice counterpoint to the richly hued, furniture-style island designed to match the dining room cabinet.*

Spanish Colonial Revival (1910–1935)

Spanish Colonial architecture arrived before any other colonial style, taking hold where the Spanish settled, primarily in Florida, Texas, California, and the Southwest. Houses were of adobe; some were of stucco-covered stone. Their windows were small and unglazed, and roofs were either flat or low-pitched.

Spanish Revival style is a romantic recollection of the architecture of those colonial settlements. Never a national style, it flowered in areas of Hispanic roots during the era of period revivals, 1910–1935. Despite the breadth of influence and their geographic dispersal, Spanish Revival homes share many common features. Azulejos, the brightly glazed tiles of Spain, decorate doorways and stairs; wooden entry doors are sometimes intricately carved; and figural wrought-iron railings grace balconies. Courtyards are prevalent, taking advantage of the style's prominence in temperate climates, as are arched openings. By 1940, the style's popularity waned, though it survives in isolated communities, such as Santa Barbara, California.

ABOVE: *The garage and its driveway divided the house from its yard.* **RIGHT:** *The back of the house opens to a garden and presents a serene face. By following the design rules of the older house, this addition becomes its complement.*

LEFT: *Covered by the master suite above, the covered porch looks out to the private garden. The new garage, now detached, is both a pleasant backdrop and an effective screen from neighbors' yards.*

there wasn't enough salvaged hardware for the new windows, the architect chose oil-rubbed bronze surface latches and bolts similar to the original hardware instead of standard casement-window cranks.

TASTE AND SENSIBILITY TRIUMPH

The owner's new home, about two-thirds larger than its original size, is a triumph of taste and sensibility in a time when ostentation frequently overrules both. An attractive front elevation is largely unaltered by a masterful application of the architect's craft. In the back, an unremarkable house is completely and beautifully transformed.

BEAUTY IS IN THE DETAILS

British Arts and Crafts · Chestnut Hill, Massachusetts

Architect Mies van der Rohe said, "God is in the details," meaning that if we attend to the details, then beauty will blossom. In this 1906 Arts and Crafts home, the details add up to a wonderfully balanced composition. The original rooms are finely finished, and the carpenter's pride in the work is obvious. It's easy to see, too, that the owners took equal care throughout every step of the project.

Although the original house looked large, there were few rooms. On the first floor, large living and dining rooms flanked a broad stair hall, behind which lurked the Scrooge of all kitchens. The owners enjoy cooking and entertaining, and they wanted a more suitable kitchen. They also wanted a cozy room downstairs where they could retreat. On the second floor they wanted another bedroom, a new master suite.

Architect Jeremiah Eck worked with the owners to design an ell for the new rooms using a design vocabulary reflecting their informal use, while maintaining harmony with the formality of the original house. The owners studied precedents, read books on the Arts and Crafts movement, and went to see exemplar houses. Their most significant visit was to Naumkeag, a Shingle style mansion in Stockbridge, Mass., designed by Stanford White. From Naumkeag, the owners and Eck borrowed form and style for their own project. In particular, they were impressed by the simple beauty of the kitchen and butler's pantry, both rooms of natural wood and with

Life slows down in the den. Symmetry prevails, lending a quiet, relaxing environ. Mahogany wainscoting encloses the room for intimacy. Art Nouveau details, such as the fireplace surround, tie the room to its Arts and Crafts roots.

FIRST FLOOR

Den

Kitchen

Breakfast

Mudroom

Dining room

Living room

SECOND FLOOR

Master bedroom

Master bath

*All paths lead to the kitchen. The den,
nearly hidden behind the kitchen, is
anchored by a large fireplace.*

minimal moldings. Borrowing this look, the new first floor rooms are natural wood, matching the dining room; the new bedrooms are painted wood, like the other second floor rooms. For continuity, they chose a few simple trim profiles, mostly rectangles.

CREATING A SPECIAL DESTINATION

The jewel of the addition is the den. Located at the rear of the ell and removed from the formal rooms, it is a retreat. To make the den special and private, Eck tucked its centerpiece–a Rumford fireplace–out of view from the adjoining kitchen. Only upon entering the den are you awed by the tall, Rumford fireplace, with its distinctive herringbone firebox. Windows wrapping the corner opposite the fireplace fill the room with light and provide views of the yard and patio.

The den is well proportioned: each side 15 ft. in length, with an 11 ft. ceiling, two feet taller than the original rooms. The high symmetry–length, width, and height nearly the same–provides a restful balance. The den's features, from ceiling beams to bookshelves, and picture rails to mantels, all fall along rhythmic patterns. Such organization encourages one to pause and relax.

LEFT: *The original house looks big, a scaling trick created by a broad wall and heavy wood trim.* BELOW: *The design language of the original dining room influenced the style for the new rooms on the first floor.*

TOP: *Instead of a wall, a china cabinet shields views to the kitchen from the stair hall beyond. Glass doors keep the kitchen feeling open and light.* FACING PAGE: *Through symmetrical windows and ceiling shape, the bed is the focus of the new master suite. Trim is carefully scaled to the room's proportion.*

Stained mahogany wainscoting blankets the room in warmth. Simple moldings of understated scale complement the depth of the woodwork. Art glass accents bring sparkle to the rich wood tones—cabinet doors of leaded glass with bull's-eye highlights and clerestory windows painted with floral forms—thoughtful touches that introduce the craftsman's hand where you might not expect it.

ELBOW ROOM

The kitchen, between the old house and the den, is the hub. Adjacent to it are a new mudroom, a reconfigured laundry room and butler's pantry, a patio, and the den. An ingenious plan cuts a potential Gordian knot of traffic. Careful placement of doors and openings define two paths clearly, no matter what your destination may be. The new ell-shaped kitchen is to the side. It is functional, comfortable, and sized to meet the owners' needs.

GETTING THE BALANCE RIGHT

The new master bedroom on the second floor of the ell (on page 73) is the tallest room in the house. To lift your eyes skyward, the ceiling flows to follow the roof, illuminated by a clerestory window and banded with trim emulating the half timbering of the exterior. While this could have produced a bloated room that lacked scale, it did not. The bedroom is expansive yet intimate.

To achieve this balance Eck used two scales. One is large and meant to impress: the soaring ceiling. The other is human and meets you eye to eye. Two trim bands wrap the room, one at conventional ceiling height, the other at picture-rail height. Above the upper band, the paint changes from wheat to cream, which makes the wall seem shorter. Windows set at eye level draw your attention across the room. Two cozy niches flank the fireplace. So while the space is dynamic, it is balanced and inviting to those who sleep there.

A MATTER OF SCALE

The new ell carries forward the language of the old house. Eaves and windows align between old and new, as does the half timbering. Materials and trim are identical.

One challenge facing the architect with the ell was scale: the house is tall, and the ell, which needed to be long and narrow, risked looking awkward. To overcome this, one-story-high features were placed around the perimeter. When you enter the house from the mudroom or patio, you do so below a roof and eave that welcomes you. Also, the den's one-story bay window projects from the walls, reducing their visual height. Finally, landscape designer Robert Hanss devised a terracing of the property, visually anchoring the house to the ground and further reducing its scale. Attention to details underlies the success of this stunning addition.

2

CREATING
PUBLIC
AND PRIVATE
SPACES

"In remodeling the old house...there must be a careful study given to preserving the atmosphere of the old work, for old houses often have a character and charm not to be fully expressed in words."
−John Calvin Stevens

We've looked at how your addition and house must be designed in balance with each other and how that balance is achieved. Before we discuss just how to craft the transitions between these old and new spaces, let's examine the second cornerstone in creating an old house at harmony with its new space−the role of public and private rooms in an old house. Much less important in a house that was built after 1940, old houses were designed with a clear hierarchy of space. Because we're talking about rooms, we'll be focusing mainly on the interior of the house in this chapter.

Old houses have a dignity arising from a clear ordering of rooms. I liken it to a dress code in which public rooms are black-tie affairs, while private rooms are no-tie-required. Rooms in historical floor plans are arranged to create

Raised panels are a hallmark of formal rooms such as this dining room. A large crown molding, chair rail, and baseboard contribute to its dignity.

In a 200-year-old back hall, far removed from the public eye, the wall finish is basic: tongue-and-groove pine boards (some with knots), a modestly-sized baseboard, and no window casing.

an experience: to entertain, to impress, to wine and dine, and to relax. And rooms are ornamented for the experience intended. When designing an addition to a historical home, I strive to preserve this dress code and the original dignity of the house. I seek to understand the original role of your old rooms before considering how they can be used today and how the rooms of your addition should interact with them.

In this chapter we shall consider such questions as how old rooms should function in conjunction with their just-built counterparts and how new rooms should be finished. By now, it should be no surprise that the best way to think about such issues is by taking our cues from your original home. Let's look at how the basic floor plan functioned for any old house built in the golden era—from 1740 to 1940—and then see how to add to it.

THE ROLE OF ROOMS

Like anyone contemplating adding on to their home, you're thinking about how your house is now and how you wish it were different. For those who live in old houses, this becomes a complicated proposition. You don't want to strip your home of its integrity, yet you need to create space for the way you use your home today. There's a history here that should not be ignored.

In America, the earliest colonial homes typically had one all-purpose room. However, rooms were added rapidly and became specialized. As the number of rooms grew, it became increasingly difficult to keep an entire house warm,

FACING PAGE: *The parlor is one of the earliest public rooms. The farmer who built this late 18th-century room spared no expense to impress his friends. After all, the parlor sets the bar in décor; no new room should rise above it.*

especially in New England winters. Walls and doors were built to separate rooms from one another so that closing off nonessential rooms concentrated the heat to key rooms. This compartmentalization of homes was encouraged further because it was in step with the increasingly formal social etiquette of the period.

The earliest specialized room to evolve was the bedroom, soon followed by the kitchen, both of which were considered private and were placed to the rear or side of the central room. When there was sufficient space under the roof, bedrooms were also placed on the second floor, though it was common for one bedroom to remain on the first floor, perhaps to care for the infirm. The kitchen commonly had a buttery–equivalent to a pantry today–and a borning room attached. The borning room was a small room for the birthing and care of infants. It opened onto the kitchen to capture

This late Georgian bedroom evolved more recently into a suite, gaining extra floor area from the move of the adjoining bath and closet to a small addition.

This powder room is both utilitarian and stylish. A vanity is assembled from found objects of simple design. The plumbing is left exposed, but finished in unlacquered brass that will slowly turn a rich brown similar to the antique floor.

its warmth and allow the mother to attend to her baby while preparing meals in the kitchen.

The parlor and dining room developed next. The parlor was a public room to receive and entertain guests. As a public room, it was placed at the front of the house. The dining room, too, was a public room that hosted guests and family, and took the family out of the kitchen for meals, a desirable choice then.

THE EXPANDING AMERICAN HOME   By the early 18th century middle-class homes might have four to six rooms on the first floor and up to four bedrooms on the second floor. To make it easier to move between rooms and floors the central stair hall took shape, with the stair frequently a showpiece that greeted guests arriving at the front door. A selection of these rooms, plus servants' quarters in larger homes, defined the floor plans until the 19th century when, as our nation prospered, further room specialization occurred.

By the early 19th century, members of the genteel class eager to display their erudition needed libraries. Typically, their libraries adjoined public rooms. By the mid-19th century, the stair hall grew to become a living hall. More common in late Victorian homes, it recalled the grandeur of the great halls of medieval Europe. Stairs filled one end of the living hall to greet guests entering opposite at the front door. The parlor, dining room, and library flanked the living hall for an impressive public display.

Also at this time, doors between public rooms were replaced with cased openings. This opened the procession through the house and improved light and ventilation, concepts that people were beginning to embrace toward the end of the 19th century.

One of the last rooms to be added to a home, the bath first appeared mid-century in high-style homes, but was not common until the 20th century. Some

While converting rooms on the second floor do not be tempted to change the stairs. I consider the original set of stairs sacrosanct. The materials and craft that went into making it cannot be replicated today without significant expense. And, today's building codes often require that the new stairs have a gentler run to rise ratio. Some designers recommend replacing an old stair balustrade with a new one matching that of a new stair in an addition. I don't. If a new stair is a part of your addition, it will nearly always be placed in the informal section of your home and therefore *should* be different.

The formal stair is crucial to the second floor, funneling the family together every morning. In fact, there was a special stair layout common to Federals called the "good-morning stair" because it gathered the family onto a common landing before they descended to begin their day. In the design of your addition, try to keep the new rooms on the second floor connected to the old stair. It's still a place for the family to connect.

early models of Sears and Roebuck kit houses did not offer a bath at all. Plumbing was a modern convenience that did not reach across the classes until about 1920.

With the 20th century, the role—and the number—of rooms further changed. New American house styles like Bungalow, Prairie, and Craftsman tended toward a smaller repertoire of rooms. The collection of public rooms the Victorians enjoyed—parlor, living hall, and drawing room—was consolidated into a new room, the living room, which tended to be larger than the parlor but was otherwise a formal public room for guests. The dining room remained a formal room, and the kitchen continued to be a private room tucked out of sight.

ABOVE: Baths were a modern innovation in any old house, so there's much leeway in the way they are treated in a home today. Here, a bath accommodates a window pattern on the facade of an addition to a Georgian home. FACING PAGE: *This addition expresses our lives today: Rooms open to one another to encourage easy movement about the house. Openings of various widths lead views from the kitchen to the new rooms beyond: a breakfast room, mudroom, family room, and screened porch. Opening widths vary to both highlight social centers, like the kitchen, and obscure private zones like the mudroom.*

The stair hall returned to a more modest size, but remained the most common way to introduce guests to a home, with the stair as showpiece. Cased openings continued to be used, and in some high-style examples partitions were eliminated between public rooms, creating open floor plans for the first time. Frank Lloyd Wright's Prairie style houses often lacked partitions, using only floor level changes and centrally positioned chimneys to delineate public rooms.

These stairs are a study in contrasts. The stair shown above, original to an early nineteenth century farmhouse, stands ready to greet guests. It's craft was intended for display. The stair shown on the facing page, part of an addition, is hidden behind a bookcase so the owners can secret away to their private study unnoticed.

MOVING AROUND THE HOUSE

Today, the way we define and use public and private space in our homes is in transition again. Guests feel comfortable wandering around areas that were strictly off-limits in the past, and are as likely to retire to a stool in the kitchen as they are to settle into a wingback chair in the living room. Families often eat in a breakfast room, not the dining room. And, even though more of the house is open to guests, there are more rooms that are intended only for the family and close friends, including the family room, breakfast room, mudroom, sunroom, media room, master suite, guest suite, home office, exercise room, laundry room, and game room. Where should you put them? To design a floor plan I assign rooms to one of three categories, which I call conversions, adjacencies, and separators. Most new rooms are informal, and all can be seamlessly integrated with their original structure with thoughtful planning.

CONVERSIONS An old house's best guarantee of survival is to adapt it so that it will be enjoyed today as it was before. Rooms that are no longer functional should be converted to new spaces– this is an opportunity to create room without having to go to the expense of

RIGHT: *When you are converting old rooms to new, it's surprising what space you can find. A built-in by a window in an old bedroom becomes the perfect home office nook. The conversion works well and acts as a buffer for the new bedroom beyond.* FACING PAGE: *The living room of this Prairie home is large and open to the foyer beyond. Along with the dining room (out of view), it accounts for all of the formal, public space in the house. Although Prairie houses are more relaxed than their Victorian predecessors higher craft is still displayed, from the coved ceiling to the paneled wainscoting.*

adding on. For example, the multiple parlors of Federals, Georgians, and Greek Revivals are excellent candidates for conversion. As they tend to be small and adjacent to each other, I often recommend removing the wall between to create one larger room more appropriate for entertaining today. Not only does this revitalize your house, it saves your money.

This works well when looking to create a new formal, public room, such as a living room. In such a case, I choose a parlor of comparable formality, one that is accessible from the front hall and shares the front elevation. The same concept works well for a new family room, a room that must sit halfway between public and private. Instead of using a front parlor, I combine two parlors to the rear. This places the less formal family room in a more private setting, appropriate for its use.

The Second Floor The second floor of most old houses is filled with bedrooms, a reflection of a time when families were large and inter-generational living was common. The second floor is as private today as it was long ago. It is rare for guests to be invited to the second floor unless staying with the family. Your second-floor addition should continue as a collection of private rooms. Any number of new private rooms can be converted to a spare bedroom. Other rooms that are appropriate for the second floor are home offices, playrooms, and sitting rooms, which have become popular with master suites and often double as exercise rooms. In my house, we have converted one bedroom to an office and another to a playroom for our two children.

A spare bedroom can also be converted to two smaller rooms, for example a laundry room and walk-in closet. Avoid, however, dividing any room if that would affect the window placement on the original facade.

A new master suite, which requires about the same floor area as two bedrooms in an old house, can get an assist from a spare bedroom. If you have two adjacent spare bedrooms, you may be able to create a master suite from them without an addition.

ADJACENCIES   In plain English, an adjacency is the most basic of additions–it's a room or rooms literally added on to the old house. As we have discussed, old houses are not flawless. The three most common complaints I hear are that there's no room for casual living, there's not enough natural light, and it's hard to enjoy the backyard. Some rooms destined for the addition address these deficiencies when placed adjacent and open to the old house. Let's look at each old-house deficiency and the new rooms that can correct it, and how these can be put adjacent to the original house without breaking the public/private dress code.

The Kitchen Today the kitchen is more often the hub of family life, the center of our casual lifestyle, a place to visit with guests while preparing meals. And our appliances and

FACING PAGE: *As the stair ascends from the second to third floor, the balusters change from turned to simple square and the decorative skirt scroll stops. A simple newel post marks your arrival at level three.*

gadgets were simply unimagined by our ancestors. It is no surprise, then, that the kitchen is the most frequently renovated room in the house.

I usually expand the kitchen from its original location as a means of preserving its historical placement in the house. Despite its central role, today's kitchen is still an informal room and would be out of place among the formal rooms of your home. I restrict views of the kitchen from formal rooms, such as the parlor or stair hall, but open the kitchen to adjoining private rooms, such as a family room, to encourage conversation during meal preparation.

Connecting with the Backyard Other rooms appropriate for an adjacency are those that connect to the backyard. Today we relish our backyards as extensions of our indoor rooms, for the woods beyond them, a view of a city skyline, a private terrace, or an outdoor grill. But historical houses were disconnected from the backyard. When they were built, the backyard was likely filled with a barn, farm animals, the privy, or the summer kitchen. The backyard was a place to avoid when enjoying the company of family or friends. Today, however, we embrace it.

A mudroom is one way to connect your house with your backyard. It is a small, but hardworking room, the cloverleaf interchange of the house. I like to face the mudroom toward the backyard to make it easy for family to reach the yard. Also, your yard will be more enjoyable if you have a place for muddy boots and muddy paws to track in without angst.

The Family Room   The family room is another candidate for connecting to the backyard and can loosen up almost any home whose collar is a little too stiff. I place the family room near the stair hall for easy accessibility, and off the rear or side of the house because of its informal role.

FACING PAGE: *Breakfast rooms are new. Lined with windows that face the back-yard, this one uses the simplest of details to create a quiet, inviting place where pajamas are welcome.* RIGHT: *This mud-room is functional and fun. Built-in cub-bies for each child make the room lively and efficient. The beadboard wainscoting is able to take more abuse than plaster and it adds a little character.*

I like placing new family rooms next to the backyard, because doing so connects two informal, but socially active areas. Also, placing the family room in a rear addition frees it from the stricter geometries that govern the front facade. French doors, taboo on a front elevation for a transparency that is too informal are acceptable on the back of an addition. Use them to invite guests to enjoy your outdoor room.

SEPARATORS   Certain spaces in additions are best placed away from the public areas of a historical home, because they are private rooms, such as a bedroom, or because the activity they will house is disruptive to the order and ambiance of an old house. Consider the garage. When possible, I place the garage away from the house. Five homes featured in this book have detached garages, four of which are placed in the rear corner of the property to good effect. When attached, as I've discussed in the introduction, keeping the doors away from the facade is critical. If attaching your garage, locate the doors to the side or rear.

CREATING AN ELL   If you position your addition so that an ell shape is created with the original house, it provides a cozy embrace for a terrace. As a model, consider the Italian piazza, whose allure is in part from the protective security of the building walls that define it. By having two informal facades facing onto the terrace, there is opportunity to place larger windows and doors in several rooms looking onto the terrace. This improves natural light in the house and provides several new ways to reach the outdoors.

Houses whose long facade faces the rear yard are conducive to an ell plan because the addition can be placed to one end and perpendicular in axis. Federals, Tudors, and Shingle styles often have long front and rear facades that work well, whereas Greek Revivals and Bungalows typically have narrow faces and may have awkward proportions if contorted into an ell. If you own a home with a narrow face, consider instead placing a garage addition to the rear corner of the property. Use a breezeway or mudroom connector between house and garage; a lovely, private courtyard will appear.

ADDING LIGHT

Perhaps the most common complaint about old houses is that they are dark. Up until the mid-19th century, architectural styles never grouped windows. The

concepts that guided the design of Capes, Georgians, Federals, and Greek Revivals forbade grouped windows. If you see grouped windows in one of these homes, it is a sure indication of a recent change. And it was rare for a wall in a room to have more than two windows.

Further dimming the interior was the tendency to use small windows on the back of the house. Glass was expensive in our early history, and rooms where views and natural light were not a priority were put in the back of the house. Besides, few wanted to gaze upon the privy or the barnyard.

Despite the absence of historical precedent, I include light-filled rooms in my additions because our backyard spaces have evolved into extensions of

our homes. I place rooms such as breakfast rooms, sunrooms, and conservatories to the rear of a house, or to the side but well back from the front facade because rooms full of windows take on an uneasy, contemporary look next to a historical facade.

Breakfast rooms and sunrooms are informal, private rooms meant for the family or close friends. They are adaptable to any traditional style. Because the idea is to add space as well as light, I make sure that the doors or cased openings connecting these rooms to the original house are generous. I keep both rooms small to create the intimacy becoming an informal room. I like to place these rooms on a corner, where at least two walls can be filled with windows, giving the room a porch-like feeling.

A conservatory is a special public or private room, an architectural jewel. It's comfortable in a variety of roles, from

ABOVE: Adding an ell to the back of a house often results in a backyard that beckons, creating just the right scenario for a patio. FACING PAGE: *Views are a priority for this sunroom, which looks out onto the Atlantic Ocean. Windows wrap the room, and muntins are excluded in favor of an uninterrupted horizon. An expanse of glass, without muntins, is acceptable on the back of a house.*

Sometimes a kitchen, to function properly, is out of scale with the other rooms in a house. In styles inherently modest in size, such as Bungalows or Capes, an imposing kitchen can upstage an adjacent formal room and create an awkward transition from old to new. A design trick to consider for reducing a kitchen's apparent size is to install cabinets that are not uniform in design; rather, they are arranged as in a collage.

The effect is analogous to a large room that is empty versus the same room filled with furniture. An empty room is uniform; you can take it in all at once, which can make you feel small standing in it. In the same room filled with furniture your eye moves from object to object, leather chair to upholstered sofa to wooden coffee table so that the room never feels bigger than the area to which your attention is held.

formal dining room to private garden retreat. Its history extends back 300 years in Europe. And though in the United States conservatories have played only a bit part in the design of most historical homes, over the last 20 years the room has grown in popularity. Conservatories are costly, but worthy because they can add a powerful infusion of natural light. A conservatory's striking form can be easily tucked to the rear as a private oasis or placed prominently at the side in public view.

DRESSING A ROOM FOR ITS USE

It might be too harsh to say our ancestors were social climbers, but certainly many of them loved to display their wealth in ways that implied high social status. Rarely was money spent where visitors could not appreciate it. This attitude prevailed throughout the golden era, and was applied with conviction to room finishes. Rooms intended for guests were formal and the finishes were the best the owner could afford.

Floor-to-ceiling raised panel walls were common in the public rooms of Georgian and Federal homes. Floors of parquetry, an expensive geometrically patterned wood inlay, adorned Victorian parlors. Redwood paneled walls with high plate rails warmed Craftsman living rooms. The ornamentation in private rooms was simpler or even absent.

Federal owners were bolder. Interior doors commonly had raised panels with a delicate molding wrapping the panel perimeter on the side facing the parlor or dining room, while the opposite side of the door–out of the public realm–was a basic recessed panel without molding. These split personality doors were used on closets and between the parlor and stair hall, with the hall getting the plain face because it wasn't considered a formal room.

In general, we don't make houses as we used to. After 1940, the population exploded and a housing crisis spawned whole towns of instant, mass-produced homes. They lacked the prevailing craftsmanship or high design of the earlier era. And there was a breakdown of decorum. Public and private spaces in a home were never again to be so distinctively set out. But for those of us who love houses that predate this

FACING PAGE, TOP LEFT: Stucco is solid, uniform, and clean, and suggests refinement, even in a simple building such as this carriage house. **FACING PAGE, TOP RIGHT:** *Tucked in the corner of an ell, this conservatory addition to a Federal home is filled with light and views. Reclaimed limestone pavers connect the room to the landscape.* **FACING PAGE, BOTTOM:** *Exposed boxed beams, chair and picture molding, and sophisticated window trim work were meant to be appreciated in formally accoutered rooms such as this Federal parlor.*

period, we should try to retain those age-old distinctions between public and private, formal and informal rooms.

PUBLIC AND PRIVATE MATERIALS   For homes built before 1940, there is a hierarchy among materials, and inside the home wood sits at the top of the list. Wood was the material of choice for formal, public rooms. The finest woods were used, chosen for their durability, appearance, and sometimes scarcity. For example, those designing Georgians preferred pine. It could be cut in very wide boards and was easily shaped with hand tools into raised panels and moldings. Victorian and Craftsman designers preferred white oak for its durability and natural beauty. In the formal rooms it was quartersawn, a choice cut with a beautiful grain. Western bungalows leaned toward redwood.

Exit the public rooms and a change is quickly apparent. Victorian floors change to tongue-and-groove heart pine, then to open grain plank flooring. Walls of paneled oak give way to wallpapered plaster, then to the simple painted pine beadboard common to kitchens. Bungalows may have a high, formal redwood wainscot in the living room, a lower wainscot in the dining room and no wood paneling at all in the bedrooms. Baths were tile–utilitarian. Federals featured full height, raised-paneled walls in the parlors but plaster walls everywhere else.

Trim   Trim is another chapter in the story of a house's progression from public to private. Public rooms through the end of the 19th century, and in certain 20th-century revivals, had a combination of crown moldings, picture rails, chair rails, and baseboards. Window and door casings were intricate, often with a back-band molding to give heft. Baseboards were tall and capped with a molding. Balusters were turned to a delicate profile. Spanish Colonial Revival and Craftsman homes relied less on trim to ornament a public room, making use instead of coffered ceilings and exposed trusses to awe a guest.

Beyond the front rooms, the trim changes. Moldings become smaller and simpler. In a Colonial Revival home, the living room might have an antiquity-inspired crown molding 12 in. tall, but the kitchen will have a modest crown 3 in. tall, and the bedrooms may not have a crown at all. Some moldings only appear in the most formal rooms. Chair rails are rarely

The formal stair hall is finished in stained wood. The balusters and newel post are turned and intricately carved. Painted trim in the room beyond signifies its less formal status. The door between the rooms is painted on one side, stained on the other. The more formal finish, in this case the stained wood, always takes precedent along the door edge.

seen outside the parlor and dining room. Casings in a Victorian throttle down from a broad, backbanded molding, to a belly casing in informal rooms, and flat stock in attic rooms.

Finishes After the mid-19th century naturally finished wood–stained, waxed, or varnished–was the uncontested favorite finish of formal rooms. If an owner could afford a nicer species of wood and the better cut, it was shown off by a transparent finish. If wall paneling were beyond the budget, the trim–casings and baseboard– would be naturally finished in the parlor or living room.

Wallpaper also graced formal rooms. For more modest homes where large areas of wood was not possible, wallpaper covered the surfaces. By the Craftsman

Master bedrooms are private, with less ornamentation than the public rooms. The floor of this
bedroom is heart pine and the trim is painted, typical of informal rooms. But the room is elegant, too,
with its dramatically tall and narrow French
doors and hefty baseboard.

era William Morris had transformed wallpaper designs into graceful organic patterns that were sought after. For Craftsman homes wallpaper features were sometimes used in the same way as a crown molding was used in a Victorian home. In private rooms both plaster and trim were painted.

OUTSIDE MATERIALS   There is also a formality hierarchy among exterior materials, which is used to differentiate formal public facades from informal private facades. At the top of the ladder is stucco. For centuries in Europe, brick and stone facades were not considered refined and were coated in stucco. Although that trend had passed before American architecture thrived, stucco remained the material of choice for many styles. Not until 20th-century revivals was stucco commonly used on more modest homes.

Stone closely follows stucco in formality because of its sense of permanence, cost, and the skill required for assembly. In its most refined state, cut stone with tightly fitted joints surpasses stucco.

Brick is a step down from stone. It is still a formal material, but with less of a sense of permanence than stone. Houses built of bricks of uniform size and color, laid with thin mortar joints, have a more formal appearance than those of less uniformity have.

Try as it might, wood never assumes a more formal role than stucco, stone, or brick, but it can still be a formal facade material. Yet, it is equally appropriate for the shed addition off the rear ell. At the most formal end is shiplap siding, the version with a deep shadow line. Shiplap with only a modest shadow line becomes a degree less formal. Comparable in formality is clapboard siding, with narrow spacing that becomes more informal as it widens. Quickly descending from there are vertical tongue-and-groove, shingles, and board-and-batten.

The purpose of this hierarchy is to define the relationships between materials, not to assign a value to your home. For example, a Federal style home finished in clapboard can be just as formal as a Romanesque home of brownstone. Materials of similar quality are more compatible than those that are not. When considering your addition, this becomes

A collection of materials intersect where old and even older meet. The brick of the eighteenth century summer kitchen is comfortable next to the shiplap of the house, which has a beaded edge for added formality.

important because historically it was common to use less expensive materials on the back and sides of the house. "Why spend the time and money on a wall that will impress no one but you and your family?" was a common mind-set.

If your addition is to the rear, or telescopes to a modest single-story, consider changing the materials to reflect its less formal role. Choose a material from the hierarchy that is below but near the original material. For example, adding a rear ell clad in clapboard would be appropriate for a brick Federal style house. But, using board-and-batten siding on the same brick house would be inappropriate because of the disparity in their craft and refinement. For a more detailed discussion of materials, see chapter five.

CONTINUING THE STORY

The story of a historical house's public and private rooms is an important feature of all old houses. We may be moving away from the rigidly defined public and private lifestyles of the original inhabitants of these wonderful homes, but it doesn't mean we can't incorporate the spirit of the past and make our own spaces wholly livable.

LEFT: *The irregularly-shaped stones around this entry, with pillowed, or rounded, faces give it a rugged, solid feel. The door is set well back of the stone face to accentuate the stone's mass.* **ABOVE:** *Clapboards wrap the public facades of this Federal style home while shingles are used on the back wall. The one-story addition also has shingles, and a small lean-to is basic board and batten.*

FOURSQUARE AND MANY YEARS AGO

American Foursquare · Washington, D.C.

MaryAnn and Rick Nash's Foursquare is well-proportioned, has interesting details such as diamond-pattern windows, enduring materials like a slate roof, and elegant public rooms arranged about a stair that flows like a bride's train. They love their old house and for many years resisted the need to expand it. But the backyard was difficult to reach and seldom enjoyed, and the kitchen was isolated and dark. There was no place to unwind, because all the space besides the kitchen area was used for three public rooms: a stair hall, a living room, and a dining room. Upstairs, the master bedroom was the largest room in the house but the bath was cramped and the closets were minimal as if to say, "Welcome, but don't stay long."

The Nashes aired their grievances with Ralph Cunningham, an architect experienced in getting the most out of an old house. They concluded by saying how much they liked their home and insisting that what was right must not be wronged by an addition.

Ralph saw that the house was not undersized as much as it was disorganized, especially the informal areas of the house. With the exception of the new family room, most of the Nashs' problems could be solved by reorganizing the floor

The Nash's Foursquare presents a formal face, governed by symmetry and finished with stucco. Placing the addition in the back of the house did not alter the historical home's character.

The old floor plan had a procession of formal rooms but an informal family area was missing. In the new plan, the addition to the rear provides ample room for a new family room. The kitchen grew enough to include banquette seating for informal meals. A new screened porch off the back is accessed from the kitchen and family room.

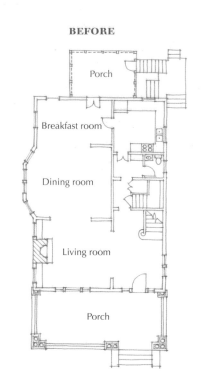

BEFORE

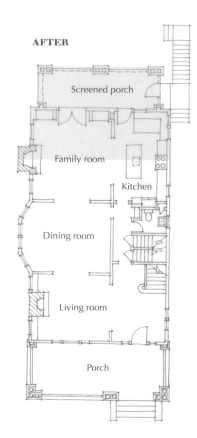

AFTER

plans. Ralph studied various plan arrangements and found a solution that minimized new floor area and left all of the rooms at the front of the house untouched, preserving the facade from unwanted window changes and preserving the public procession of formal rooms.

The first floor now has a 10-ft. addition to the rear where the new family room is located. It's placed along the back wall and through a pair of French doors, opens onto a new screened porch and the yard beyond. Adjacent and open to the kitchen, it creates a strong link between two informal, but highly active, contemporary rooms. The renovated kitchen, residing in its original location, is now bright thanks to two additional windows, a French door to the porch, and the removal of an interior wall. The bond between the kitchen and family room is reinforced by a reorganization that puts an island with a sink centered in front of the family room fireplace. When working at the sink or preparing food at the island, the cook has a generous view into the family room.

FACING PAGE: *The stair hall is a graceful introduction to this home. Beyond, a French door hints at the private yard, but gives no clue that the new kitchen is adjacent. Decorum is preserved.*

BRINGING IN LIGHT

Originally an uninviting hall behind the stair led to a kitchen door. The door was removed in favor of a cased opening of the same size. Beyond, at the back wall of the kitchen, the new French door aligns with the hall, making it lighter and more inviting. The hall also opens to the old dining room. When serving meals in the dining room the bustle passes through the hall, not the family room. These simple changes enliven the hall, separate the kitchen from the formal entry, and ease the flow among all rooms.

It can be hard to accept making a room smaller in your house. It feels like a step in the wrong direction. But a

OLD HOUSE STYLE American Foursquare (1900–1930)

American Foursquare is a subtype of the Prairie style and became the most popular vernacular expression of that movement between 1900 and 1930. The floor plan of a Foursquare is, not surprising, usually square with four rooms over four rooms. The roofs of these two-story homes are low-pitched and hipped with large overhangs. Most feature a hipped dormer on the front. The facades are symmetric with a prominent front entrance, frequently to one side. Almost all have one story front porches. Wings were single story and clearly subordinate to the square mass. In the vernacular versions, the windows are usually double-hung.

The Foursquare offered the most house for the money at that time. Sears Roebuck offered Foursquare house kits for $1,995. Near newly established rail lines, entire neighborhoods might be of this style. In these years of period revivals, Classical, Italianate, or Mission trappings adorned these simple structures.

LEFT: *As a reward for converting a part of the master bedroom to a bath and closet, the roof of the first floor addition is now the floor of the master suite's porch. A half wall wraps the porch for privacy and provides a sense of embrace. The ceiling is pleasantly high and in scale with the porch.* **ABOVE:** *The new rear facade is different from the front facade in all ways but one: elegance.* **FACING PAGE:** *Preserving the order of rooms is important. As seen from the dining room, the new family room and kitchen make for an open and roomy tandem. The island screens the messy activities of the kitchen. Walls and openings are placed to control views and make it comfortable to move about.*

deficiency in an old house is not always best answered with an addition. The architect saw that at the second floor an addition wasn't necessary. Instead, he made the bedroom 8 ft. narrower and used that area for a new master bath and walk-in closet. Because no floor area was added to the second floor, the roof of the addition below is now a screened porch for the master suite. This is a nice consolation for allowing the bedroom to shed a few unneeded feet.

Today, all that was right about this Foursquare remains so; the façade will continue to turn heads as it has done for nearly a century. Inside, the classic procession of formal to informal rooms can still be enjoyed. And, the Nash family can now enjoy living in the house as much as owning it.

EMBRACING A
BOLD IDEA

Federal · Chester County, Pennsylvania

Home owners David and Canby Page are not afraid of a bold idea. When architect Peter Zimmerman proposed moving their old Federal farmhouse and turning it completely around in order to accommodate the addition they had in mind, they were all for it. These were the first steps of a well-executed renovation that preserves the stately character of their period home and creates a new living experience inside and out.

The house rests on gentle hills that have been cultivated since the area was settled. Tucked in the hills is a handful of barns that once supported farming and now support an equestrian avocation. The house faced the barns and, despite a plenitude of land, was crowded against the road. It had its complement of formal rooms—a stair hall, two parlors, and a dining room—that were all original to the house. The kitchen was a 20th-century addition that was poorly proportioned and placed. Any change would include its removal.

The Pages wanted a mudroom, laundry room, family room, and an airy kitchen with ample counters. They also wanted a terrace that felt a part of the house but offered panoramic views of their land. For a family that enjoys their land as much as their house, the house offered little connection to the land. Upstairs there were sufficient bedrooms but only one bath, and the master bedroom had a small closet, typical of the period. They wanted a contemporary master suite.

The formal stair hall opens to the private rooms beyond and begins the procession through the house. A family room window at the far end invites one along.

The ell of the addition is located to the rear to preserve the original rooms and their use, and to create a private patio where the family can relax during summer evenings. Doors from the parlor, kitchen, and family room open to the patio. The kitchen opens to both the stair hall and dining room, and separates the formal rooms from the utility rooms.

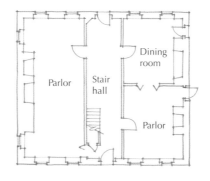

BEFORE

AFTER

Family room

Kitchen | Laundry

Terrace

Porch

Dining room

Parlor | Stair hall

Parlor

Dining room

Parlor | Stair hall

Parlor

Parlor

RIGHT: *The historical house stands proudly on a knoll, with the addition placed quietly behind. All features of the facade are preserved including the trim and windows. Three new dormers are symmetrically placed along the roof to heighten the facade's formality.*

FACING PAGE: *The original dining room is rich in details that make it formal, including a crown molding, a chair rail, oak floors, and an ornate mantel. It is frequently used because the new kitchen is adjacent.*

TURNING ITS BACK ON THE LAND

Zimmerman moved the house into the landscape and turned it 180 degrees so that the back was toward the barn and the front toward the lawn and approaching drive. This set the stage for the addition. Because the new rooms are private, Zimmerman placed the addition behind the house as an ell, a traditional solution. This preserves the taut front facade, which is well proportioned and perfectly symmetrical.

The addition unfolds in steps, first in the stucco of the main house, then to less formal clapboard. This visually breaks the new structure into pieces leaving the main house dominant. Nestled in the ell and hidden from the street is a terrace that opens to the landscape on two sides. Five French doors open onto the terrace from the addition, plus two doors that had been windows in an old parlor. Leaving the house to explore the grounds is now inviting and easy.

The addition is an ell that opens up to the property and to views of its agrarian history. A pleasing sequence of materials begins with stucco at the main house, clapboard at the last section of the ell, then simple tongue and-groove boards at the old barn. From the patio, friends and family can watch the owner school her horse.

RIGHT: *The master bath is finished to look like other private rooms of the second floor, with pumpkin pine floors, and trim of the same size and shape.*

BELOW: *The kitchen is spacious and inviting. Cabinets have raised panels like the original house, but smaller moldings of simpler profile than those of the public rooms. Cabinets undulate in depth and height to give them a built-in appearance and avoid a contemporary look. An opening in the wall connects the kitchen to the family room.*

Returning to the front facade, Zimmerman made one change to reinforce its public persona by adding three dormers along the gable roof. The change is effective as it makes the house appear taller. The original facade had a minor slouch, with the horizontal eave of the roof resisting the chin-up proportions of the windows. The dormers carry the vertical posture above the eave, lessening its influence.

Inside, new and old meet twice on the first floor, once at the stair hall and once at the dining room. Both openings were there originally. The kitchen and family room line up behind the stair hall, creating a long procession from the front to the back of the house. The kitchen also opens into the dining room.

The family room is at the back of the addition, separated from the historical house because its character is very different. Stepping down from the kitchen, it opens up under a cathedral ceiling. The room is pleasant, even fun, because of its height. Also separated from the old house are the new mudroom, laundry, powder room, and family entry. They are grouped and placed next to the kitchen.

Because of the limited connection between old and new, the historical rooms were at risk of abandonment. To preclude this, the formal stair is maintained as the only stair, so that to reach the second floor one must pass through the formal area of the house. Also, there is no breakfast seating area in the kitchen. You can pull up a stool at the island, but all meals are served in the 200-year-old dining room.

Upstairs the new master bedroom and bath are in an addition over the kitchen. A pre-existing bedroom is converted to a small office for the suite, and separates the bedroom from the stair hall and other bedrooms. Behind the house, the master bedroom has views across a magnificent landscape, one of the many rewards the Pages received for embracing a bold idea.

OLD HOUSE STYLE Federal (1780–1820)

Archaeological discoveries at Pompeii in the mid-18th century provided the clearest vision ever of Roman domestic architecture. English architect Robert Adam studied the ruins and lead a design style evolving out of Georgian that came to be known as Adam or, in the United States, Federal. The Federal style resembles Georgian: high symmetry governs, the entrance is the centerpiece, windows are ungrouped, and classical details embellish facades. However, Federal facades have more delicate proportions and are less elaborate.

The proportional shift is most obvious in the slender muntins. Higher interior ceilings also made facades taller. Window height followed suit, with larger panes made possible by glass production advancements. The roof is often low pitched. Federal architects employed curved lines, such as elliptical transoms over the entry door, and Palladian windows placed on the second floor above the door. Oval and circular rooms also grace some homes of the Federal period.

FROM CHAOTIC TO CASUAL AND COMFORTABLE

Cape Cod Revival · Bethesda, Maryland

Two empty nesters, Bob and Anne, wanted to simplify their life. The understated, even straightforward look of this Cape Cod style home caught their attention, but the location is what grabbed them. A large backyard, and downtown shops and restaurants within strolling distance, made them fall in love with the house.

The inside, on the other hand, was more like a funhouse than a home. A bedroom opened to the foyer, and the kitchen and family room were on opposite sides of the house. Rooms were closed off from one another, making a modestly sized home seem downright small. And the backyard was ignored. Bob and Anne couldn't live in such chaos. They wanted a comfortable home that promoted a casual lifestyle. At the top of their list was a family room that connected with the yard. Both having careers in academia, they wanted a library for their extensive book collection. Finally, a private study for each of them would put the home in concert with their lives.

The new floor plan, designed by architect Jane Treacy, is tightly organized with a procession that would make a Victorian proud. But it is also open, with multiple views carefully framed that encourage flow and make the house feel roomier. Along the back is a large family room addition, full of windows and doors. Off one end is a screened porch. Off the other end is a study, reached through narrow openings on either side of the fireplace.

A new family room takes advantage of its private setting and stretches its design legs. It is large, sized to be the social center of the house, and the barrel-vaulted ceiling gives the room height proportional to its size. A ribbon of windows warms the family room with the colors and textures of the garden.

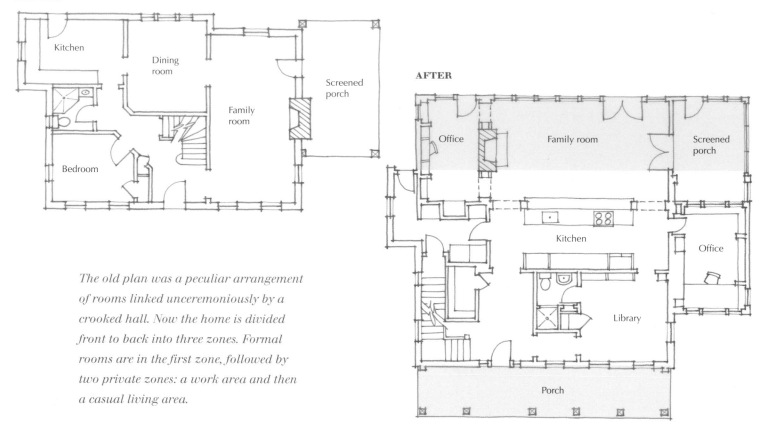

AFTER

The old plan was a peculiar arrangement of rooms linked unceremoniously by a crooked hall. Now the home is divided front to back into three zones. Formal rooms are in the first zone, followed by two private zones: a work area and then a casual living area.

The middle of the house is a work zone. The kitchen is galley style, one long side open to the family room and its outside views, the other a wall full of appliances and cabinets. The mudroom is along a short side separated by a door. The second study bookends the mudroom and converts an unused porch. A small vestibule between the kitchen and study gives it breathing room from an otherwise imperfect adjacency.

MAKING ROOM

The front zone of the house is formal. The original stair was moved, a difficult but necessary decision because its S shape made it hard to use and its central position hindered room size and flow. Now to one side the stair flows into a commodious foyer sized to receive guests comfortably. From the foyer, a view to the private zones of the house is controlled through a line of openings that lead to the garden beyond. To the side of the foyer is a new library accessed through an

ABOVE: *The library is tall for its size giving it a formal feel. It opens to the private rooms through a narrow opening, so it is separated but not excluded from their activities.* **LEFT:** *The Cape has a new front porch the width of the facade to express its formal role and make the approach more inviting. Set back to the right was the old porch that is now a private study.*

anteroom that augments the formal procession. Secluded and without any modern media, the library is in the spirit of 19th-century parlors where conversation among friends was the focus.

Outside the changes to the house are modest yet effective. A porch was added along the front. Classical details harmonize with the Cape's colonial roots. The porch softens what was an abrupt facade and offers protection from weather. The side porch that became a study is finished in clapboards, a comfortable step down from the more formal brick of the main facade. To the back and out of view is the addition. Covered with a shed roof, it is a simple form appropriate for a rear addition. Stretching from end to end is a row of windows, punctuated with French doors. The casual conclusion to this quiet Cape has Bob and Anne embracing it as home.

FACING PAGE: *The galley kitchen shares views of the garden with the family room. Conversation can flow easily between the rooms, but a wall set above counter height blocks views of messy preparations. The kitchen is designed compactly because no paths go through it.*

LEFT: *The home owners can comfortably greet guests in their new foyer. The opening to the private rooms is wide enough to entice but narrow enough to maintain the foyer's ambience.*

A BAY AREA BEAUTY

Prairie Style · San Francisco, California

When their family grew, the owners of this two-story 1909 Prairie decided their house had to grow, too. They wanted a one-car garage, a contemporary kitchen with natural light, a guest suite, a master suite, and a media room. The site—a steep, narrow lot—severely limited their options, but it provided dramatic views of San Francisco. They decided to stay put, face the challenge, and add to their experience by playfully exploring new materials and finishes.

Architect and friend David Gast designed a modest ell set back from the front and finished the space that had been a walk-out basement. Converting the basement preserved the scale of the house and saved money. But only certain rooms will work in this least ceremonial and most separated part of the house. Gast placed the guest suite and media room there, giving both rooms windows and French doors opening to the backyard. He put the garage at basement level in the new ell and next to it a mudroom.

Tasteful styling need not be reserved for public rooms. This kitchen is dramatic despite its simple details. Straight faces and square edges define the cabinets and the counters. The two-tone painted cabinets and the oil-rubbed bronze hardware enliven the room.

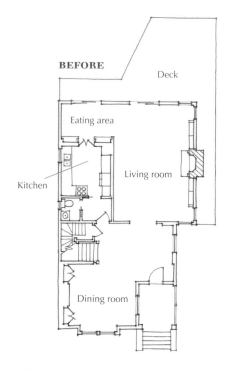

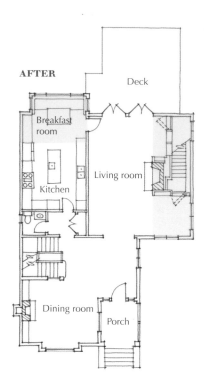

The new plan preserves the order of rooms. The kitchen is now functional and open, with a bank of windows overlooking San Francisco. The ell extends the living room and gives shape to a quiet reading nook.

The owners kept the formal look of the public spaces on the first floor, where the original dining room, foyer, and living room are preserved. They are open to one another, in character with the Prairie style and appropriate for public use. The living room, which is larger, benefits from the ell addition. It now has an intimate reading nook. Wainscoting wraps the rooms and is painted white like the trim. The floor is white oak with walnut borders. Plaster walls are rich colors, their visual weight reinforcing the formality. Ceramic tiles in geometric patterns of saturated colors surround the fireplace.

A NEW COOKING SPACE

The old kitchen was small and closed off, the stunning skyline hidden. Its one window faced a neighbor. There was room for one cook, who could not converse with guests when preparing meals. Gast expanded the kitchen from its location to the side of the public rooms, taking floor area from the breakfast and living rooms.

The banquette is invitingly scaled and affords its occupants ample sun and city views. Separated by a door from the living room, the pleasure is private—for family and invited guests only.

Now the kitchen is an attractive destination. It reaches the back of the house, concluding with banquette seating wrapped by windows. Floor-to-ceiling cabinets surround the work area. The banquette is painted beadboard, and the cabinets are faced with a simple recessed panel. The floor is a pattern of light and dark cork tiles. In contrast to the weighty color of the living room, the kitchen is painted a bright informal combination of yellow, sage, and cream.

Upstairs, the old master bedroom demonstrated that more space does not make a better room. It was 25 ft. long, but had four interior doors, a 5-ft. cased opening, and bump-outs that left the owners wondering where to put their bed. Gast used that area plus a few feet of the ell to create a new master suite, an office, and a child's bedroom. The master bedroom is 10 ft. shorter, but with only two thoughtfully placed interior doors the room works. A bath and closet complete the suite. Both bedroom and office are lined with windows overlooking the city.

The master bath is a room of wonderful materials, a private oasis for the owners. They lined the walls with tongue-and-groove Port Orford cedar, covered the floor with matte tile hand-glazed in azure blue, and capped the vanity and soaking tub with two kinds of limestone. It is elegant and memorable.

Outside, the ell adopts the language of the old house. Red cedar shingles in alternating wide and narrow bands cover old and new, emphasizing the horizontal lines of the Prairie style. Both garage and sloping drive are invisible from the street. The ell is so quietly added to the old house that it would be easy to pass by and not notice the change. This ingenious addition is restrained and maintains the distinction between public and private areas. It respects the character of the historical house.

ABOVE: *Baths are good places to experiment. This master bath uses materials unique to the house but respects the spirit of the house. The cedar walls emphasize the horizontal lines of the Prairie style. The vanity is free of mouldings, like the kitchen cabinets.* FACING PAGE: *To the side of the living room is a reading nook. It's a contrast in scale but remains a public room, so it's finished with formal wainscoting, weighty trim, and a coved plaster ceiling. The bookshelves to the left open to a private stair.*

RIGHT: *The historical house is restrained in ornament and modestly scaled. Its Prairie styling is defined by eaves that project well beyond the facade, a shallow-pitched hip roof, and bands of shingles that suggest strata.*

BELOW: *A mature cypress shields the new ell from view. Beyond is a hint of the vista the rooms inside enjoy. The ell adds valuable wall area to the rear elevation, which hoards the commanding views.*

FACING PAGE: *A beautifully detailed fireplace with its chunky wooden mantel and tile surround and hearth is well in keeping with the Prairie Style aesthetic, which highlighted natural materials and craftsmanship.*

Prairie Style (1900–1940)

Around 1900, a group of talented architects led by Frank Lloyd Wright put a clean sheet of paper on the drafting table and developed a uniquely American architecture: Prairie Style. A declaration of American architectural independence, these architects did not look to Europe for ideas. Nor was reviving the past their business. Originating in the Midwest, Prairie homes formed in response to and as a part of the landscape in which they were built. Low-pitched hipped roofs with deep overhanging eaves project from the house like the bill of a baseball cap. Bands of casement windows, cantilevered rooms and balconies, and long, narrow Roman brick further emphasize the horizontality. There is minimal ornamentation, and natural materials are emphasized.

Inside, the houses followed the belief that well-designed living space would improve the quality of family life. For Prairie school architects this meant floor plans with few interior walls. These homes feature rooms open to one another and overlapping each other. Prairie style homes also break down the distinction between interior space and exterior space by using glass walls and enclosed balconies. A massive chimney at the center anchors the one-with-nature structure in place. Although out of favor by the mid-1930s, Prairie style remains an American original.

3

MAKING
THE TRANSITION
FROM
OLD TO NEW

"In things to be seen at once, much variety makes confusion, another vice of beauty. In things that are not seen at once, and have no respect one to another, great variety is commendable..."
–Christopher Wren

The most common question my clients ask is, "How do I make the transition from old to new?" Whether considering the project from its exterior or interior, the question of a well-executed transition–the third cornerstone of good old-house design–is always in my mind.

While the transition is often challenging, it can be done gracefully when a thoughtful designer identifies elements that will conflict and finds ways to achieve harmony. Poor transitions create aesthetic and functional problems, and while the aesthetic issues can detract from your pleasure, with functional problems all the effort you put into creating the new space can go to waste. A common functional problem occurs when flow is affected and the new space is closed off and so is not used. The absence of thoughtful design can lead to structures in which all that was invested is lost and all that was beautiful is buried.

An old house is like a journey through time. Long hallways lead from the past to the present, from formal parlors to warm, contemporary kitchens.

We'll look at a project first from the outside and then from the inside; your home's exterior and interior are distinct domains, each with its own requirements, which, at times, may conflict. For example, putting your new garage on the right side of your house might be the very best location as viewed from the street, but it would not be acceptable if that arrangement had you entering your home through your formal dining room.

THE EXTERIOR

When I design an addition, the entire exterior presentation of my client's home comes into play. I take time to walk the property, looking at the house, imagining various shapes and locations for an addition. Unless it's a particularly unusual setting, one of three basic approaches will work. I call these telescoping wings, connectors, and roof raisers.

ABOVE: *The brownstone portion of this New Jersey home was built in the 1790's, and consisted of a parlor and bedroom. Later, a dining room was added, then a kitchen, and finally a storage room. The additions, in less formal clapboard, create a pleasing telescoping wing.*

FACING PAGE: *Varying rooflines and a clever palette of materials camouflage the many transitions between new and old in this Pennsylvania farmhouse.*

THE TELESCOPING WING   Many historical houses, especially those in rural New England, were expanded with a telescoping appearance. Houses grew one simple addition at a time, one piece behind the other, diminishing in size as they progressed. These wings off the main house formed roughly an "L" shape in plan, which gave rise to the word ell for all extensions off the original house, even those that did not form the L shape. The ell preserved the formal facade

Out of Focus Telescope

A telescope addition works best when its roof pitch matches that of the original house. In this example, the telescope and its porches assume three different pitches and take on an expression of their own. Where one would expect the roofs to step down in an orderly manner, they fall asunder. Odd-shaped wedges of wall separate rooflines, and the top of the porch roof almost hits the low gable roof.

of the original house because it was typically located to the side or to the rear. These additions appeal to me. Their warm, even idyllic, charm is the result of an organic, unpretentious, and straightforward approach to the down-to-earth human needs of the moment.

The telescope addition can be an effective design approach for your home. It can incorporate a lot of new floor area without overwhelming the original house or announcing to the neighborhood that you have just doubled the size of your home.

So that it doesn't interfere with the original facade, the telescope usually steps back from the front of the house, reducing views of the addition. If you step it back far enough, it allows you to place a farmer's porch in front of your new facade. This porch, when applied to a two-story facade, further diminishes the apparent size of your addition. It also creates a perfect spot for your porch swing, boot scraper, or tea table and, if properly oriented, shades rooms from the summer sun.

The telescope addition can host an assortment of rooms because its shape is so flexible. Family rooms, sunrooms, kitchens, and mudrooms are commonly included. Kitchen and family room additions are sometimes large enough to overpower the original house, but their size can be well-masked in a telescope. Also, these rooms tend to be more private and often benefit from access to the backyard. The master suite is another room well-suited to a telescope. Today, many people prefer their master suite, which often has a walk-in closet and private bath and sitting area, to be a bit separate from the rest of the house, near but not within the fray of family activities.

ABOVE: *A rambling addition extends off the back of a Queen Anne, following the steep grade of the site.* FACING PAGE: *The porch to the right is set well back of the front facade, preserving an original bay window. The new porch shares its design vocabulary with the original beyond, but the diameter of its columns is smaller to be in proportion with its more modest size.*

RIGHT: *A connector can be subtle, as it is on this Federal farmhouse. The original gable, to the left, stands clear of the addition to the right, separated by a connector that is lower and set back.* FACING PAGE: *A Federal style house and barn are joined by a connector. Smaller than the buildings it links, it shares a vocabulary with both buildings: tightly spaced clapboards that match the house (and are more formal than the barn's more widely spaced clapboards), and a porch that segues to the barn's arcade.*

THE CONNECTORS   A connector links the original house to a second structure in a modest way. It is like an elastic material binding two large objects together, while being stretched as needed to allow the addition to be well placed. Historically, breezeways are the most common connectors, linking the carriage house, stable, or barn with the main house.

A connector may provide nothing more than a path between old and new, but it might also serve as a mudroom, a gallery, or a conservatory. A connector can be open to the air or be enclosed. It can have its own recognizable shape, such as an arcade, or simply fill the gap between buildings. It is a device to link rooms and activities.

If a connector is the best means for adding to your house, pay careful attention to the siting of the addition; it must not compete with the original house, and rarely should the addition extend as far forward as the front of the original house.

An Attached Garage   The garage is almost a necessity in a 21st-century home, and its size means that it cannot be overlooked. But, that doesn't mean the garage must dominate the scene. A connector allows you to disengage the garage from the body of the house and to place it in an appropriate location, usually to the side and rear of the main house. (For more about garages, see chapter three.)

Outdoor Spaces Connectors can also be used to define outdoor spaces. As neighborhoods grow up around old houses that were originally in rural settings, backyards tend to lose their privacy. A perimeter fence, opaque and tall, can be a quick fix, but I try to avoid this solution. It shields your beautiful home from view and can set an unfortunate precedent along a block of beautiful old houses.

A connector can define and screen outdoor space while preserving views of your house. For example, in one project where the home owner wanted to link his house with a detached barn, I designed an arcaded breezeway, approximately 25 ft. long, which provided shelter and closed off a corner of the yard previously open to the street. The result was an ell-shaped arrangement of main house, connector, and barn that shaped and cloistered the backyard without blocking the street view of the house.

GOING UP If you have considered—and rejected—the telescope and the connector, you may want to consider expanding upward, even though it is the most difficult way. Consider for example that most towns and cities have zoning bylaws that limit how near your house can be to your property lines. On a small lot, expanding upward may be your only possibility. Another common reason for expanding upward is to preserve your yard. In my neighborhood, where lot sizes are in measured square feet, many home owners would be loath to forfeit any yard space. I utilize three design options when I see that the only place to expand is vertically—using either dormers, remodeling the roof, or actually raising it.

Adding Dormers The most common way to gain a room in an attic is to remove a small portion of the roof and insert a dormer under which you will create usable floor area. Chances are, if your house has a sloping roof, adding a dormer is an option. This relatively easy change can enhance the character of your home and is common across nearly all styles.

Dormer shapes are as varied as the roofs they sit on. They can be features of a design, such as an eyebrow dormer; they can support the design by repeating expressions elsewhere, such as gable dormers that align with pedimented windows

Connecting an outbuilding to a main building is historically how most golden era houses were expanded. Seeing it done today, here with a monitor to vary the roofline, creates a new house that appears as if it hadn't been added on to for 150 years.

The Roof as a Tool of Transition

Three components of a roof indicate the formality of the space below: the ridge, the eave, and the rake. The highest ridge will be over the most formal facade. As the roof makes the transition to your addition, it is preferable that the new ridge be lower than the original so that the main roof remains dominant. At the bottom of the roof is the eave, projecting beyond the facade anywhere from a few inches to a couple of feet. The eave's height above the ground is significant, the most formal facade of the house having the highest eave. For a proper transition, aligning new with old is common, as is dropping the new eave.

If the new eave aligns with the original, it should have the same moldings. If your addition is to the rear or has a lower eave, you might simplify the molding or eliminate it. The more the rake—the roof edge revealing the slope—projects beyond the wall, the more formal the look. Similarly, a rake with moldings is more formal. Across most styles, the rake is a small, flat board on rear ells or one-story telescope additions.

below; or they can recede from view, such as a shed dormer tucked into the back corner of a roof. Consequently, dormers can alter or reinforce the architectural expression of a house. I often use them to gain a little space for a getaway room such as a home office. I find the flexibility of their form appealing and handy when I want to reinforce a home's character. But be careful in your choice; make sure the dormer is in harmony with the language of your house. And don't be greedy; a common mistake is to add a long shed dormer to a delicate roof line. While this adds considerable floor area, it can destroy the line of the original roof.

Remodeling the Roof Not all old houses were well-designed, and the roof form is a common culprit. I recently worked on a 200-year-old home that was originally part of a fishing village at the mouth of a river. The house was charming and modest—a simple rectangle 20 ft. by 50 ft. Because it had only two bedrooms, the occupants—a family of four—needed more space. The roof, an inappropriate and unattractive shallow pitch gable, was their only option. I designed a gambrel roof, which allowed me to add a master suite with commanding views of the river.

Raising the Roof This approach differs from a roof remodel in that the entire roof or a major portion of it is lifted, creating taller walls below it. This will likely provide more floor area than other roof changes, but it will also affect most of the design elements of your house, from frieze boards to wall area. Juggling the changes to so many building components while preserving your home's balance can be daunting. It's important to take the utmost care.

First, don't completely erase the lines of the original house. Try not to alter the eave (the lower horizontal edge of a roof) along the front of the house. This is possible for side gable homes, such as Colonials and Bungalows. Another approach is to introduce a lower roof; for example, a covered porch in front of the taller walls to lessen their visual impact. The style of your home will dictate the best approach.

ABOVE: *The shed dormer on this Tudor home shows off its craftsmanship, with copper downspouts, exterior panels, and perfectly scaled brackets.* **ABOVE RIGHT:** *A hip dormer adds visual interest to the roofline and square footage inside.* **RIGHT:** *Shed dormers along an ell create an undulating eave pleasant to the eye. Because the dormers pop up above the eave it makes the size of the ell look smaller. One long shed may have been easier to build, but it would have made the ell out of the scale.*

Cupolas and Monitors

Another option for changing the roof and gaining headroom and floor space is to add a cupola (below) or monitor (right). Monitors are long and rectangular and sit on the roof ridge. They have windows along their long sides. Because they run along the top of a roof, they are best when used on simple roof forms such as gables.

Cupolas are focal points upon roofs where the roof shape is a crescendo leading to the cupola. Both monitors and cupolas are common across several styles; the character of your roof and the style of your house will suggest which is more appropriate for your home.

LEFT: *The taller addition, beyond, is masked by the cascading tile rooflines of the original house in the foreground.*

THE INTERIOR

It may seem that the most difficult part of adding to your home involves the exterior when the interior is, in fact, what will be most profoundly affected. After all, you'll be living there. This is your chance to update the flow and function of your old home, to make it a beautiful, sheltering place that not only nurtures but also inspires you. On a practical level, this is your opportunity to fix problems. For example, in old homes, kitchens were often small, dark, and isolated. With an addition, you can create a kitchen that not only connects with the old rooms but also is also large enough to eat in.

Fortunately, though the challenges of making the interior transition from old to new are many, you can enjoy the exercise, because you will have at your disposal many powerful tools for this work. Perhaps the most powerful of these is room size. If your family room is overflowing when your growing family gathers, now is the time to push some walls around.

Another powerful tool is room arrangement. I call the passage through the rooms of a house, procession. Maybe the procession through your home is a little boring. If so, you may want to create a surprise or two so that your guests won't anticipate what's coming next. A cathedral ceiling in a house of 8-ft. ceilings adds interest and drama to your procession. You have many other tools to create the character of the inte-

THE ART OF CRAFT — Replicating a Gutter and Downspout

Carpenter Al Grover welcomed the job of replacing the gutters and downspouts on this British Arts and Crafts home. The original wooden gutters were unlined and rotten, and the lead pipe downspouts had deteriorated. On the gutters, Al used redwood for its rot resistance, and glued and nailed the pieces together in a jig of the correct profile. He also lined the gutters with copper, using a hand brake to shape the metal. He soldered all joints then added a copper drip edge, securing the gutter to the eave with metal straps.

Each downspout had a bend in it, called a gooseneck, bringing it close to the house wall. Although lead is pliable, every time Al tried to bend the pipe it would buckle. He found the solution in the back of his truck: a vacuum hose that fit into the pipe. Al inserted the hose, packed it full of damp sand, and plugged each end. He then bent the lead pipe around this jig for a perfect gooseneck.

FACING PAGE: *This new master bedroom stands apart, but not cut off, from the old house: A short hall opens onto the main stair. The bedroom has a tray ceiling, which allows the roof to be lower outside. As long as the flat portion of the ceiling is at least 8 ft. 6 ins. high the room will remain spacious.* **RIGHT:** *Sometimes public and private meet at inopportune places, such as this corner where the formal hall and back stair meet. A corner bead, in the natural wood of the hall, comfortably transitions wallpaper to paint, and natural oak to painted poplar.*

rior. These include trim, wall finishes, flooring, lighting fixtures, windows, doors, and hardware.

In historical homes, the layout of rooms was structured to support the formal manner in which hosts interacted with guests. (If you've read the third chapter, you know all about public versus private spaces.) Old houses, especially those built before the 20th century, were divided into distinct rooms with limited connectivity between them. Given today's more informal lifestyle, you may wish to break down the distinction between rooms. And, if you decide on an open layout for your addition, you will need to create an attractive transition between it and the tightly controlled procession of your old rooms.

The decisions are many as you set about designing the interior of your addition, but there are three basic decisions that, correctly made, will ensure a functional and pleasing interior that respects and engages the interior of the original house. You must decide how and where to join the new to the old, how to size your new rooms, and how to finish them.

ABOVE: *A tall, narrow cased opening leads from the dining room of this Georgian to the new stair beyond, and a floor material change marks the transition. By keeping the opening narrow the informal character of the stair is kept out of view of the formal dining area.* **LEFT:** *Standing in the original living room of this Foursquare, openings are aligned and wide to the addition beyond. It is easy to move about this house.*

LEFT: *Tucked behind the kitchen the pantry opens to the new mudroom, its French door bringing sunlight to the prep area. A bar sink and wine storage serve the family room behind. This service area is both handsome and functional.*

FOLLOWING SPREAD, LEFT: *New and old meet quietly in this sunroom addition. The sunroom, adjacent to the dining room inside, opens to the old veranda and the backyard. Perfectly placed, one doesn't realize how small the room is.*

FOLLOWING SPREAD, RIGHT: *The connector between this original Georgian in Connecticut and the addition is an innovative window bridge—instead of hiding the connection, the architect made it an architectural element.*

HOW AND WHERE TO INTRODUCE THE NEW TO THE OLD Because you will want to move about comfortably between old and new, the interior of your addition must have a substantial connection to the interior of the original house. If it does not, this new part of your house will inevitably see little use.

When I am designing the floor plan of an addition I look for areas of the original house where the walls can be opened without damaging the original room. Such areas are convenient places to connect new with old. Also, I look for compatibility between old and new rooms that will encourage interaction between them and promote circulation. A prime example is placing a new family room next to an enlarged kitchen where homeowners enjoy entertaining and cooking.

I want new and old to blend with one another by selectively opening the old part of the house to allow the addition to be seen and used. For example, if my clients enjoy entertaining, I'm going to make sure that the new dining room is not only close to the old living room, but separated by a cased opening of generous width. However, here you may encounter a creative tension between access to the new and preservation of the old; if your home is a Bungalow, for example, with a living room of beautifully paneled walls, you will not be content to destroy an entire wall for access.

A shed roof addition gave the owners enough space for a private office, without major changes to the roof shape.

There is no set place in an old house to locate an addition. Your choice will depend on the rooms you are adding and the layout of your home. For example, if you are adding a library, you may want to put it next to the old living room. A new mudroom could go next to a back stair or hall. Look for solutions that promote the use of all rooms, old and new, while preserving the integrity of the original rooms.

Just as there are no firm rules for where to make the connection, neither are there firm rules for how to make the connection. How easy should it be to see into and walk between old and new? How much of the old wall should come down to welcome the new addition? I approach this decision conservatively, trying not to remove any more of the wall than is necessary. I think of it as pulling back the curtain just enough to reveal the stage behind, but no more. The principal architectural tools for pulling back the curtain are doors, cased openings, and portals. Each provides a different feel.

FACING PAGE: *Viewed from the original house this new second floor wing is layered in its openness. In the foreground a sitting area is open and surrounded by books, very inviting. To the right is an office, shielded from view but with a broad opening. Beyond, separated by a portal and door, the bedroom asserts its privacy.*

Doors Doors, of course, maintain the separation of the wall but allow movement between rooms in a controlled way. In communal or public spaces, I use them sparingly, if at all, as they inhibit movement. But, of course, a door is imperative to separate private rooms like a master suite addition or rooms that need firm separation, such as a garage or media room.

Cased Opening A cased opening, essentially a doorway without a door, is a common way to link new with old. Like doors,

cased openings do not extend to the ceiling. They can be as narrow as a door, and similarly restrictive, but they can also be nearly as wide as the rooms they separate, creating an open floor plan while still defining a separation between rooms.

Cased openings are also a clever way to allow adjacent rooms to differ in character. For example, ceiling heights may change between old and new. Cased openings, because they are not full height, can inconspicuously accommodate the transition. They also allow for easy transitions between finishes. Your old dining room may have rich trim, such as a crown molding, that you do not want to carry into your new breakfast room. The cased opening allows this. Similarly, a cased opening allows for a graceful transition between rooms painted different colors.

Portals   If doors are equivalent to "stop" signs, and cased openings are "welcome" signs, then portals are the "yield" signs of room separation. Portals are open and trimmed like a cased opening, but are deeper like an abbreviated tunnel. They add drama to the experience of passing between rooms. Portals have weight; they compress you for a moment then release you into the spaciousness of the room you enter. Vestibules, airlocks, and even porches, all portals of a sort, often have low ceilings so that when you pass through them and enter the home, they heighten the excitement of the larger rooms beyond.

Formal stairs of old homes will sometimes have landings under which you can pass. This deep opening, a portal, frequently separates the formal foyer and flanking parlor from the private domain of the kitchen beyond. Portals can be used to accentuate the formal procession between rooms. Walls are thickened and sometimes lined with bookshelves and displays or covered with panels to announce to your guests that they've passed to another chamber in your house. As you consider whether to introduce a portal in your addition, remember they are best used sparingly and are most effective as a novelty. If they are overused, your home will feel like the residence of a burrowing animal.

A portal separates a home office from the family room. Taking advantage of its depth, display shelves are recessed into the portal.

HOW MUCH ROOM IN YOUR ROOM?   How large should the new family room be? Is bigger better? Can oversizing a new room compensate for older rooms that are undersized? What makes a room feel right? Expanding your home should produce new rooms that are pleasant and functional.

For a room to be pleasant it must be balanced and in harmony with the rooms preceding it. To paraphrase Goldilocks, your room should not be too long, too short, or too wide. Getting it "just right" usually involves trial and error. Start by considering rooms you like, such as at your home and homes of your friends. Then measure the rooms you find pleasant.

Ceiling height will influence how you experience a room. Many older houses, especially those built after the turn of the 19th century, had tall ceilings by today's standards. Nine-foot ceilings were common, and it is not hard to find homes of that era with higher ceilings. Today new homes usually have ceilings just shy of 8 ft. The loss of height dramatically alters the ambience of the rooms. Rooms with high ceilings encourage you to pause and relax; lower ceilings weigh on you as if to squeeze you through to the next room. So, it is important to consider height when designing your rooms; it is nearly as important to a room's success as its floor area.

For you to enjoy your room it must serve its intended purpose; it must be functional. A kitchen should allow you to prepare a meal with order and efficiency. Your bedroom should provide a place for your bed of choice with easy circulation on three sides. Avoid the temptation to super-size a new room. This will not provide any more enjoyment than buying a shoe bigger than your foot. A room

FACING PAGE: *The living hall took shape during the Victorian era. In this 1885 house the living hall is an impressive display greeting arriving visitors, and a far cry from the early stair halls of the eighteenth century.* LEFT: *A deep portal provides clear separation between the master bedroom in the foreground and the stair hall beyond. The ceiling is lowered, but vaulted, a special introduction to the owners' domain.* ABOVE: *Bedrooms should be designed knowing where the bed will go. Here, high windows are spaced apart for the bed, which is symmetrically placed. The bed fills the room while not feeling cramped. The bedroom is sized appropriately.*

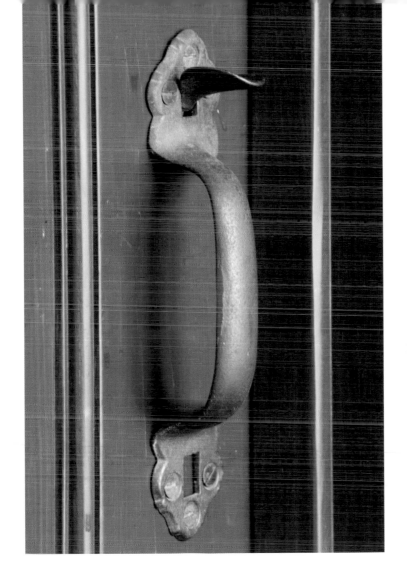

FACING PAGE: *A sitting area doesn't need to be sized as a room to be inviting. Here, a hall niche is big enough for two cozy chairs, table, and reading lamp. The window is oversized for the seating group, increasing the niche's appeal with light and views.* LEFT: *A salvaged iron thumb latch has a dull shine from use. Its patina helps the stiff new door find its place in time.*

stretched beyond your need can be hollow and empty, deadened when it should be expressive and lively. These rooms consume funds that otherwise spent could provide the fine materials, finishes, and craft that would make living in your home a lasting pleasure.

THE FINISHING TOUCHES   If you aren't aware of the breadth of artifacts that can be found in an old house, a trip to a salvage shop will be an enlightening experience, and fun, too. There you will find countless hinges, doorknobs, escutcheons, newel posts, balusters, mantels, sconces, ceiling medallions, sash locks, and more. The artisanship that went into the making of these pieces makes them timeless. Some version of many of these artifacts can be found in your home. They can work together to give your house and individual rooms the character and beauty you love.

Budgets   Fortunes can be consumed finishing a room. Even though I am regularly involved in the selection of hardware, trim, and moldings, I continue to be astonished by their cost. Fortunately, good products at reasonable prices can still

be found if you search for them. And, finding them, you will be rewarded time and again by their lasting beauty. Even a door hinge matters.

A hollow-core wood door prehung on plated steel hinges is inexpensive, but that door will look and feel out of place next to the solid doors in an old home. The hinges won't hold their finish or maintain the door's proper functioning. The trade-off in quality is not worth the savings. For our home, items such as these must capture the timelessness of the original, so we wait to execute a project until we have the funds to do it well. I consider my house, and the old houses of my clients, as gifts of a past generation to us.

Because old houses are popular these days, many manufacturers produce well-made products for them that can give your addition a wonderful finishing touch. Local shops are the best place to look because there is nothing like holding the item you are considering. Also, the Internet has become a valuable tool for finding well-made, reasonably priced items. I use both, and I am not afraid to buy items from across the country if they work best for my need and budget. Research the sources; ask your neighbors, your contractor, and your architect for suggestions. Then, enjoy the hunt.

FACING PAGE: *A new door that has been built in the spirit of old: well-crafted for generations of use.* ABOVE: *A 3½-ft. wide oak entry door needs a door knob to match. This knob and escutcheon do the job. Plated in nickel they are replicas of a 19th century Victorian pattern.*

A WELL-CRAFTED DREAM

Greek Revival · North Hingham, Massachusetts

The owners bought this lovely 1848 folk-style Greek Revival many years ago. The house was rich in period detail: casings, mantels, doors, wainscoting, and even the handrail volute at the entry stair were in good health. But space was a problem. The house was sized modestly; except for the parlor, rooms were small and inconveniently located one behind the other. The owners began to dream of an open kitchen and family room where they could comfortably entertain. Biding their time while they made repairs and updates, their addition took shape in their minds. Then they worked with architect Jim Sandell to realize it.

As Sandell contemplated the addition, he was convinced that he did not want to disturb the simple, elegant lines and shape of the home. A large barn of the same era and comparable charm stood next to the house, limiting the ways in which the house could be expanded. Recognizing that an expansion of either structure would alter its character, Sandell opted to gain the necessary floor area by joining the two structures using a quiet and unassuming one-story connector. The roof pitch is low; if not for a roof monitor, the new roof would all but disappear. A porch softens the connector's facade.

New and old meet in an airy transition. A section of wall was removed and the new post and beam framing extends into the ell, softly weaving together the two generations.

BEFORE

AFTER

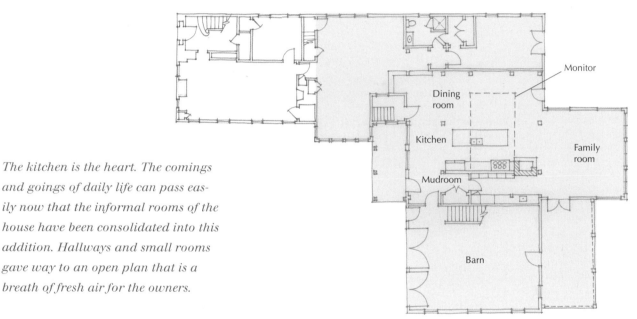

The kitchen is the heart. The comings and goings of daily life can pass easily now that the informal rooms of the house have been consolidated into this addition. Hallways and small rooms gave way to an open plan that is a breath of fresh air for the owners.

A NEW PLAN

Sandell placed the new rooms—a kitchen, family room, pantry, and mudroom—behind the house and alongside the barn. In doing so, he avoided altering the original house, while reconfiguring an ell whose rooms and layout had been ineffective. This also gave the owners easier access to their barn, which had seemed far away during New England winters.

The original dining room was converted to a casual den, and the dining room relocated to the addition. The den eases the transition between the old formal parlor and the new kitchen by separating the incongruous functions and scales of the two rooms. The den also gives guests a more intimate setting for socializing while being near the kitchen activities beyond.

LEFT: *A view from the new family room shows why this porch is getting the love it deserves. Tranquil and light-filled, it overlooks rolling fields and woods beyond.* **BELOW:** *The addition stretches discreetly between the bold forms of the house and barn, belying the dramatic changes inside.*

CREATING STUDIO SPACE

A section of the barn is being renovated as an artist's studio because the addition made it accessible, a part of the house. A new mudroom entry next to the barn allows the owners to use the barn's open space for storage. At the rear, an old screened porch hidden from the public's eye and overlooking the bucolic country-side has been given new life as a gathering place in the summer.

A HOUSE OPENS UP

Having deftly transitioned from the house on one side and the barn on the other, Sandell created in the middle a new family center–the kitchen, dining, and family rooms. No interior walls were built between these rooms, creating a beautiful space, more expansive than its square footage. The island is the center; seated there you can visit with the cook, gaze out to the backyard through the family room windows, or observe whether the mail has arrived at the mudroom door. Don't let the spaciousness fool you, this is Yankee frugality at its finest. The dining area is appropriate for its table, the family room is sized for one seating group, and the kitchen is scaled to ensure the cooks feel in control of their domain. Without walls, each room borrows space from its neighbor leading your eye to see each room as larger than it is.

OLD HOUSE STYLE Greek Revival (1820–1860)

From 1820 until the Civil War, Greek culture greatly influenced American architecture to such an extent that Greek Revival became the new national style.

Greek Revival homes are bold and confident, with trim size exaggerated to reflect Greek forms and proportions. In high style examples of the Northeast and Midwest, the pediment extends beyond the facade, supported by classical columns, most often Doric. Southern examples are the grand antebellum plantation homes with two-story columns, supporting full facade porches.

Classical Greek architecture influenced the design of every home of that period across the United States, from mansions to farmhouses. In folk versions, corner boards as wide as columns are common, as are two-part friezes with classical entablature proportions. Low-pitched roofs copy Greek pediments. Entries have elaborate surrounds composed of pilasters and entablatures, sometimes pedimented. Symmetry rules, though side hall entries are seen in more modest homes.

FACING PAGE: *Washed in light from the monitor, the broad island is the spot for watching activities. Its counter is banded with fir, a nice detail that softens the island's edge and marries it with the post and beam frame.* LEFT: *Cabinet details mirror those of the old doors.*

Open space on this scale can easily go awry, the rooms becoming long and low, the ceiling too visible. But not here. Taking advantage of a sloping site and the house's high perch, the addition's floor drops two steps, in effect lofting the ceiling. A roof monitor over the kitchen brings light to the center and breaks the expanse of ceiling, resulting in a well-proportioned, pleasant room—what the owners describe as the "heartbeat" of the house.

BLENDING LANGUAGES

With a barn to the right and an old house to the left the question is: Which holds sway over the language of the addition? The answer came easily for the owners who enjoy the character of both new and old. The addition is framed in exposed timbers reminiscent of the barn, while the details are influenced by those in the house. Out of this came an addition of simple, clean lines at once contemporary and historical.

BREATHING ROOM

Georgian · New Canaan, Connecticut

For Christine and Edward Fleischli their 18th-century Georgian home had no glaring shortcomings. They liked its location along a quiet street and had all the rooms they needed. But several small things bothered them: the detached garage was inconvenient during winter, storage was sorely lacking, and the stair was narrow and stuffed into the living room. And, though one upstairs bath sufficed, it was down the hall from the master bedroom. Perhaps one too many trips down that hall broke the camel's back; Christine and Ed woke one morning needing a change.

The Fleischlis engaged architect Dick Bergmann, who saw that the house was about one notch on the belt too small for them. There were enough rooms, but not enough space. He designed a shrewd solution: an addition of supporting functions. The addition comprises an attached garage, stair, master bath, powder room, and lots of closet space. With these fixes, the house expanded and the Fleischlis could breathe easier.

Bergmann focused on room adjacencies; after all, it was an addition of practical rooms meant to improve the utility of the principal rooms of the house. He placed a new stair next to the house, at the end of a cross hall, and opened the wall between with an inviting cased opening. The stairs rise in an open foyer so that ascending is no longer a straitjacket experience. At the first floor, the powder room is discreetly

The flat-roofed connector gently engages the old house, and the dark green trim color unites the two structures. The back of the addition frames this private garden, a sanctuary for the owners. The roof is aluminized metal, the siding rough-sawn cedar, both consonant with the barn aesthetic.

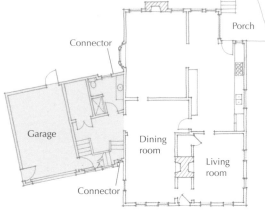

Connector

Garage

Dining room

Living room

Connector

Porch

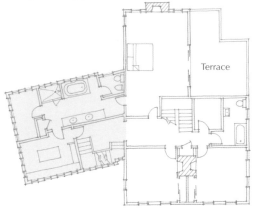

Terrace

ABOVE: *The floor plan follows the zoning setback to maximize floor area. Where new meets old Bergmann used a connector, a wedge of space that allows each a little breathing room. The new stair hall is placed at the end of a cross hall in the old house, making it easy to move about the house.*

RIGHT: *The new stair has an informal tone, with simplified moldings and painted trim. The connector is prominent, its narrow window giving you a glimpse of the old house beyond.*

FACING PAGE: *The house's broken pediment, staid symmetry, and small windows come from its Georgian roots. The addition, cloaked in a vocabulary reminiscent of 19th-century barns, stands off to its side. The small windows in the addition would be wrong for the Georgian style but are just right for the barn.*

OLD HOUSE
STYLE
Georgian (1740–1780)

During the reigns of Georges I, II, and III, a growing class of wealthy colonists built homes after the style of the great homes and public buildings then popular in England. These splendid homes embraced the spirit of the Italian Renaissance and were great examples of classical proportions, details, and ideas. Imposing, symmetrical, two-story Georgian homes sprouted from Maine to the Carolinas, varying mostly in materials. Red brick with white trim was the rule in Britain and in the southern colonies where bricks and lime for mortar were abundant. In the northern colonies, wood usually replaced brick in private residences because brick was expensive and lime was scarce.

A common centerpiece of the facade is a paneled door under an ornate pediment supported on wide pilasters. The facade typically includes four symmetrically placed double-hung windows on the first floor and five on the second. Muntins are wide, often more than 1 in. The shape of the roof varies, but usually it is modestly pitched with end gables and a detailed cornice. Dentils are often prominent. A massive chimney in the center or paired chimneys at the ends accommodate flues from fireplaces in all rooms. Interiors feature large rooms symmetrically arranged about a central hall and prominent stair.

placed opposite the stair, steps away from the dining and family rooms. The garage is half a flight lower and hidden from view but readily accessible. At the second floor, the master bedroom is now a spacious suite with bath and walk-in closets.

A COMPLEMENTARY ADDITION

Out of a narrow site and restrictive zoning, Bergmann gave shape to the addition. In contrast to the Georgian, the addition is tall and skewed from the original house, shoe-horned along the property line zoning setback. Bergmann embraced the contrast and changed the vocabulary for a distinct transition. The addition is casual and simple with board and batten siding and a standing seam metal roof. The front wall is held back from the original facade, preserving the facade's symmetry, style, scale, and formality. The timelessness of this Georgian home is retained while giving Ed and Chris the breathing room they needed.

A VICTORIAN WITH HUMILITY

Queen Anne · Lincoln, Massachusetts

For less than $1,600 a talented carpenter built this diminutive Queen Anne from stock plans in 1906. When the current owners bought the house almost 10 years ago, it had hardly changed. This was a big plus for them, as they admired the carpenter's finely crafted, delicate woodwork. But the house was less than 1,900 sq. ft. and had only one full bath. As a family of four, they needed more space. At the top of their list: a new master suite, which would free a bedroom for guests and provide a second bath. They also wanted a family room, mudroom, and a stronger connection to a spacious backyard bordered by New England stone walls and filled with songbirds.

Preserving the house's size and scale was paramount, so an addition at the rear was the way to go. But the site slopes down steeply behind the house, which is always a difficult design challenge. In such cases, too often the foundation rises to fill the void, awkwardly lifting the house away from the ground, like a boy's pants worn too long into a growth spurt. Using the drop off to his advantage, the architect stepped the addition down the hillside. The old Victorian benefited, too, because the addition, despite its size, does not compete with the house.

The new family room has a soaring ceiling, which gives the room an impressive feel. Transom windows paired with double-hung windows fill the room with sunlight and expansive views while keeping the windows in proportion with the house.

RIGHT: *The Victorian's modest floor plan is preserved. The addition is narrower and set back from the corners where it meets the older house. At the first floor, the addition has three levels that follow the sloping site. Steps between levels are organized along a circulation axis that provides long views through the house. At the second floor, the new master bedroom is separated from the public stair hall by a door and portal.* BELOW LEFT: *The addition's roofline, set below the original roof, appears to reach down to the landscape.* BELOW RIGHT: *The classic facade of this Queen Anne house was preserved when space was added to the back of the house.* FACING PAGE: *A small room with a big view, the new screened porch off the back is a strong draw throughout the warmer months.*

FIRST FLOOR

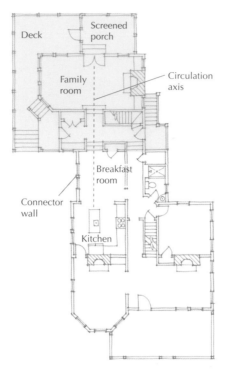

Deck

Screened porch

Family room

Circulation axis

Breakfast room

Connector wall

Kitchen

SECOND FLOOR

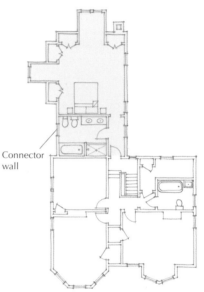

Connector wall

In the mudroom, ample trim work, here called belly casing, and bull's eye corner blocks, match the original woodwork. The door was salvaged and reused, a nice finishing touch. **FACING PAGE:** Layers of portals follow the procession from family room to kitchen. Narrow and tall, they frame views and heighten the sense of drama as you walk between rooms.

OLD HOUSE STYLE

Queen Anne (1874–1900)

Mention "colorful, fanciful, exuberant, or eccentric" when describing a style and Queen Anne comes to mind. Queen Anne is the style of "The Gilded Age," and expressively optimistic. Queen Anne began in mid-19th-century England, inspired by the multiple materials and textures, steep roofs, and asymmetry of medieval houses. American master H. H. Richardson introduced it to the States in 1874. It took off, aided by the growing influence of pattern books, and the advent of balloon framing, which made it easier to build complicated forms.

Complex organizations of roofs, walls, porches, and towers are the style's signature. Houses are lavishly decorated with factory-made architectural parts and painted with multiple colors—mostly earth tones of red, green, brown, and yellow.

Wall surfaces are highly textured in wood through combinations of clapboard and decoratively cut shingles, and in brick or stone through myriad patterns. The roof is typically steep and irregular with highly ornamented gables. Most homes have spacious porches with elaborately turned posts and balusters. At the turn of the century, Queen Anne faded as Colonial Revival gained favor.

At the juncture of new and old, the architect used a connector to separate the large addition from the old Victorian. The connector is set back from the original side facade to preserve its corner and leave the original legible.

A CASCADING PLAN

Following the lead of the exterior, the architect dropped the addition's floor level significantly below the original floor, but divided the change over three levels. This is not easy to do well; often floor level changes in homes are confusing. But here, the rooms are organized along an axis so that they cascade down before you, following the landscape until the last room, a screened porch, takes you outside. The steps provide long views and build anticipation as you move up or down.

Cased openings and portals are used to augment the procession down the slope. A wide cased opening at the back of the kitchen opens onto the original breakfast room, which was expanded by the addition. The opening masks a transition of ceiling height but otherwise leaves the rooms open to one another. A thin portal the width of a door leads to the mudroom, keeping the mudroom clutter hidden from view while maintaining an easy flow between rooms. In dramatic fashion, a deep portal compresses then releases you into the high-ceilinged family room. From there you walk out to the porch for an avian serenade in summertime or warm yourself by the fire with a hot chocolate to enjoy the views of snowy fields during winter months.

MAKING BIG THINGS LOOK SMALL

Greek Revival · northern Massachusetts

Frank, we want our house to appear as though you had never been here." The owners of this 19th century Greek Revival wanted a substantial, yet inconspicuous addition. Their antique home, sitting peacefully on the town green, had received fastidious care and few alterations. It was a gem.

But three young children made it a small gem. Add two dogs and the owners felt they were living in a dollhouse. One bath for a family of five had parents and kids lining up for the shower. They needed a master suite. They also needed kids' space: a play area and lots of storage, plus an attached, two-car garage. And, a "mother's retreat" room was imperative for an occasional escape.

To reduce the addition's bulk we designed it as a telescope set back from the original facade and stepping down in height twice. We took advantage of the sloping site and the house's high perch and put the garage half a flight of stairs below the house, allowing it to defer to the original structure.

The design uses the vocabulary of the original house, carrying windows, trim, rooflines, and their respective proportions over from old to new. Consonance was key. A scaled-down porch provides a transition from outside to inside at the new family entrance.

The telescope addition blends with the old house. It is set back behind the bay window leaving the facade to make the first impression when approaching the house. The addition uses Greek Revival details, such as the tall frieze under the roof and turned Doric columns.

SEPARATIONS PLAY A KEY ROLE

The new floor plan is efficient. A mudroom with ample storage is the anchor. Around it are a powder room, family entry, and mother's retreat. Half a flight down is the garage, and half a flight up is a cathedral-ceiling playroom. The addition contains the hustle and bustle of life and its accompanying messes, leaving the old house quieter and more relaxing.

The new rooms are sized for their function. The mudroom is all business: a long row of floor-to-ceiling cubbies, one for each family member, and a coat closet. It also provides separation between the fumes of the garage and the comforting aromas of a cooking meal. The retreat room is small—less than 10 ft. wide— and tucked to the rear where south-facing French doors and windows fill it with light. Though out of the way, it is not isolated, as interior windows and French doors look onto the family entry and kitchen. The new family entry, which joins the mudroom to the old house via a large cased opening, can be as chaotic as a Massachusetts rotary, but at 70 sq. ft., it is sized to prevent collisions.

The master suite is upstairs, occupying the taller, first wing of the telescope. There the parents can watch their children play from windows to the rear; windows to the front offer views of the town green. The master suite connects to the old house through a portal, providing the parents a private oasis without isolating them from the rooms of three active children.

Inside, we preserved all original rooms, as well as the procession through them. Outside, the complete consonance between old and new ensures that we designed in stealth.

FIRST FLOOR

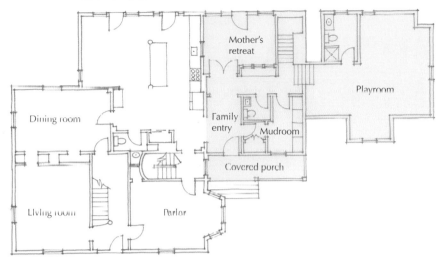

Mother's retreat

Playroom

Dining room

Family entry

Mudroom

Living room

Parlor

Covered porch

SECOND FLOOR

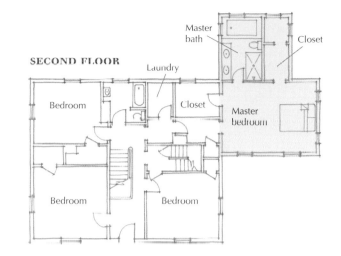

Master bath

Closet

Laundry

Bedroom

Closet

Master bedroom

Bedroom

Bedroom

The addition, comprised of private rooms, sits next to the informal part of the old house. The entry aligns with the French doors and windows of the mother's retreat, and the mudroom door aligns with the cased opening into the original house.

LEFT: The family entry opens to the original house through a cased opening next to the rear stair and kitchen. A walnut floor border and rich wall color make it a pleasing interchange. **FACING PAGE LEFT:** The historical house was graceful, but too small for the family. **FACING PAGE RIGHT:** An addition should accommodate your needs. Here a small room is a mother's getaway. It is sized for one person and given a sunny orientation.

A BELOVED TREASURE GLITTERS IN THE SUN

Gothic Revival · Sausalito, California

Architect Mary Griffin lived happily for years in the oldest house in Sausalito. A folk Gothic Revival built in 1869 it is nestled in a grove of trees beside a creek. Aside from a small shed added to the back, the house had changed little. The original center hall has a pair of rooms on either side, each of which has a 10 ft. ceiling, unusual in a home this modest.

But her house was full of doors—10 on the first floor—and felt only as big as the room she was in. Mary wanted to open up her home for views, for light, and for the pleasure of enjoying her space fully. She also wanted a new kitchen. The old one was dated and incongruously placed in what had been a parlor. Mary designed a new addition and renovated the existing space to meet her goals.

When multiple openings align, rooms frame one within the other for a pleasant effect. Through a large picture window, a mature tree appears to reflect on the fate of its cousin, now a George Nakashima table. A cased opening is all that defines the glass-enclosed sun porch, once part of the veranda.

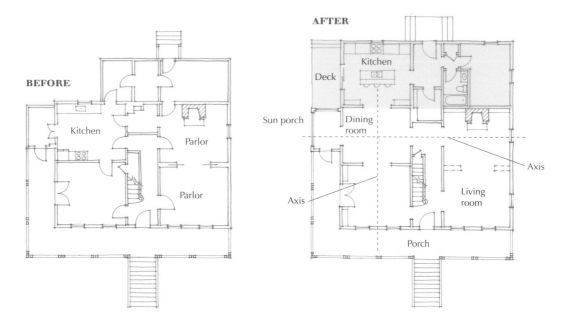

Carefully organized openings, some with pocket doors, turned isolated cubicles into a tapestry of rooms woven together by light and views.

A SHED ADDITION PLAYS
A SUPPORTING ROLE

The older shed addition was small and in poor condition. Mary removed it, but its straightforward and unpretentious character appealed to her. She replaced it with a larger shed, simple in form and details. Its overhangs are small. Its trim is smaller and simpler than that of the original structure. Its siding is a scaled down version of the shiplap on the old house. Her addition assumes a supporting role, leaving the graceful lines and proportions of her delightful Gothic Revival intact.

SMALL CHANGES
YIELD A BIG PAYOFF

Mary moved the kitchen to the new shed. She converted the vacated space into a dining room. Thus, the kitchen is behind the sequence of more formal rooms, preserving their presentation.

Also a part of the addition is a private guest suite, separated from the kitchen by a mudroom. Exiting to the rear, the mudroom is the entrance for family, a place to bring in the groceries and stow the umbrella. This comfortable arrangement of rooms resulted from considering carefully where new should meet old.

RIGHT: *The original front facade of the Gothic Revival home is nicely dressed up with a delicate porch balustrade and gingerbread trim work.* **BOTTOM LEFT:** *Though fashion and technology have changed dramatically, this Gothic Revival homestead has held steadfast.* **BOTTOM RIGHT:** *The addition rests quietly in the shadow of the house. The shed roof meets the house below the original roof, preserving its fascia and frieze board. In the foreground is a petite sun porch, created by adding two large windows between the old veranda columns. By keeping the details, including the balustrade, there is only a minimal intrusion on the veranda.*

ABOVE: *Views from the kitchen are many, making it a family center and a natural draw.* **FACING PAGE:** *Viewed from the dining room, the kitchen is awash in natural light. Translucent panels rest on traditional porch rafters, deftly weaving new materials with old. Cabinets are simple, form following function, in step with the shed enclosing the kitchen.*

The simple plan of the original house was transformed. Doors were replaced with more welcoming cased openings, sized and positioned with a surgeon's precision. Rooms with overlapping functions, such as the kitchen and dining room, have larger cased openings. Openings between other rooms are smaller, not much wider than a door. Though subtle, the variation in opening size tells the house's story: large openings encourage movement between rooms and allow one to spill into the other, while smaller openings maintain a room's separateness. All openings are organized along one of two regulating lines. It is wonderfully effective: views and natural light abound, and the house seems larger than it is.

A KITCHEN VOCABULARY

The kitchen as a center of family life is a contemporary idea. As architectural precedents don't exist, kitchens have more design latitude than most other rooms. Mary gave her kitchen a distinctive look. She used a translucent panel called Kalwall as both roof and ceiling. Supported on exposed wooden rafters the panels glow throughout the day, warming the kitchen. The room feels appropriately informal, like a back porch that has been enclosed to become a kitchen. The simplicity of the design keeps it from competing with the original rooms, while giving it its own identity.

Mary carefully transitioned from old to new. A broad opening with oversized pocket doors provides views of the kitchen while keeping it separate. New French doors and old windows are linked by using glass panes of similar proportion. The sloping ceiling is informal, yet dramatic like the high ceilings. The cabinets are simple and recede from view, and the kitchen trim is less ornate and scaled for the room. All contribute to a comfortable and unambiguous relationship between house and addition.

FACING PAGE: To the original parlor, the architect added french doors with a transom for natural light and access to the veranda. Panes are similarly sized and proportioned to the original window; the top of the transom and window align; and the door's bottom rail aligns with the baseboard. Attention to these details unifies the whole space seamlessly.

Gothic Revival started in England on the whim of an author in the mid-1700s, who renovated his house using forms and details of medieval buildings. It took root and dominated English church and government building design for the first half of the 19th century. Gothic Revival reached America in the 1830s, embraced for its romanticism and its break from the classical symmetry that had influenced building design for decades. Most homes in this style are of wood and are more prevalent in rural areas.

Gothic Revival houses emphasize verticality and the most notable characteristic is a very steep roof, with at least one gable facing the front. Almost as common are highly decorated vergeboards, sometimes called gingerbread. Other features associated with the style include pointed arch windows and one-story porches supported on tall, slender columns. Asymmetrical floor plans are the norm. The style faded in popularity in the 1860s, and few examples were built after the 1870s.

4

CRAFTING WITH MATERIALS THAT EXPRESS YOUR HOUSE'S STYLE

*"When we build, let us think
that we build forever."*
–John Ruskin

The materials of your house tell a story. A rubble-stoned Federal most likely says you're in bucolic eastern Pennsylvania. Red tile roofs and white stucco walls may say you're in the former Spanish territories of the American Southwest. In San Francisco, it's the materials, colors, and textures of the many Queen Anne houses that tell of a period of national prosperity, optimism, and self-confidence.

The materials of a house's interior are equally evocative. For example, the sensual, organic curves of Art Nouveau lighting evoke the romanticism of hand-tooled materials in Arts and Crafts homes. So it's important to study the materials in a home to learn their story, for the ones you use in your addition are their sequel.

The materials used on an old house can be as much about the house's style as the architectural elements. Clapboard, brick, and crisply painted shutters and trim clearly communicate this home's rustic Colonial roots.

Old House, Fresh Paint

For the outside of your home buy the best-performing paint available, because the real cost of painting a house is in the labor, not the paint. Upgrading to premium paint may cost more but you'll need to paint half as frequently, saving yourself money in the long run. I recommend latex and am currently experimenting with a new Sherwin-Williams® product on my house. Matching the original color is easy—most paint stores use a computer to analyze a color. Just bring in a clean sample.

I specify painting with a brush, the best way to get a consistent film over all surfaces. Because higher gloss paints are easier to clean, I use the highest gloss palatable to the eye, typically satin on the body and semi-gloss or gloss on the trim and sash.

Materials underlie a house's character and charm and are key to tying new and old together visually. The original builders chose materials carefully to achieve a goal beyond basic structural integrity–to reinforce their designs. When selecting materials for your home inside and out, do so with the same care you give to the shape and proportions of your addition.

Selecting the right materials for your addition will only strengthen the harmony between new and old parts of the house. The materials you use will be the colors and textures that give character to the new space, so it's important to choose with the same thoughtfulness you have given the space and flow of your new rooms. Just as the balance is critical to getting the form of the new addition right–respecting the separations between public and private areas, and finessing the transitions between new and old to create harmony–so, too, is selecting the best materials essential to bringing your new space together.

A fresh coat of paint on this Queen Anne not only protects the house from the elements but keeps its unique details, like the old man's face, from needing more serious "surgery."

A HISTORY OF MATERIALS

Until the mid-19th century, materials used in construction were commonly those at hand. Transportation over land was costly; moving a load of brick 10 miles might double its cost. Homes were built of indigenous materials unless a navigable waterway was nearby. Materials tied architecture to place.

The advent of the railroad in the mid 1800s changed this; materials from across the country became accessible. Machine-made parts and sawn lumber followed the railroad. Sheet metal rode the rails from East Coast mills to West Coast gold mining towns; later, redwood flowed east. Builders and architects now had an expansive palette. Architect H. H. Richardson's 1886 courthouse in Pittsburgh is clad in granite from Massachusetts, with an interior of Indiana limestone. Sears & Roebuck sold home kits that arrived to your destination in a boxcar complete with plans, instructions, and the necessary materials.

Nestled between old barn buildings, this Federal farmhouse in Pennsylvania is a study in material contrasts. Against the home's neutral stucco exterior, wooden shingle and standing-seam metal roofs are highlighted by copper downspouts.

This Prairie style house eschews the ornament of its Victorian predecessors and favors materials harvested from the region, such as western red cedar shingles.

ABOUT THE HOUSE Smorgasbord

These two houses were originally twins, but they have since taken divergent paths. The house on the left has maintained its Shingle style design; the house on the right, photographed from a similar direction, did not.

The Shingle style house uses select materials to express and reinforce its design ideas. Shingles wrap the building in a skin, and curve in a gentle flair above the foundation. Painted wood trims the porch, appropriate for the wood house. Columns are well-proportioned and the railing between them is light and airy. The foundation is rubble stone, a strong base for the house.

The house on the right is no longer a Shingle style. Victimized by random acts of clumsiness, this house is left with an identity crisis. The addition to the front obliterates defining forms, such as the shingled bracket and deep overhang, and materials have been applied to the facade without attention to precursors. White wooden blocks, emulating the quoins of Georgian houses, are lapped with cornerboards, common for many styles but not for Shingle, so that the house appears to have oversized zippers at each corner.

And the porch is given a new material—polished stone tiles—assembled 7 ft. high. Resting on these imposing walls are delicate posts whose proportion is closer to that of a baluster than a column. Collectively, these parts neither express nor reinforce the design idea of the house.

AN EMBRACE OF PLACE Despite the wide range of available materials, some architects and builders began to choose only those that were indigenous. The idea that a house should reflect its natural surroundings took hold after the Arts and Crafts movement, led by William Morris, began to gain popularity in America. Gustav Stickley, who championed the Craftsman style, believed a house ought to be in harmony with its landscape. Frank Lloyd Wright's Prairie School architecture specified the use of local materials. All the stones in Wright's famous Fallingwater came from a quarry a quarter mile from the house.

TOP: Where materials and regulating lines meet, a strong statement is made. Here, the new facade of a British Arts and Crafts house presents a strong grid of half timbering tempered by new windows.

NEW OLD CHOICES The broad palette of available materials continues to grow, but a return to using indigenous ones is under way because more homeowners are choosing environmentally friendly options. The rising cost of energy and concern over global warming are leading some to choose local materials to save the petroleum required to move materials about, or salvaged materials to save the energy of producing new. We also have more "green" products—recycled materials and hi-tech substitutes.

THE ART OF CRAFT

Making a Straight Wall Curve

Some things are harder to make than they appear, such as this curved, shingled wall. The effect looks as effortless as the molding of soft clay. Here, the skill of contractor Roger Charron was put to the challenge. First, Roger made a template for the curve, and then placed wooden studs at 4-in. intervals. In order to achieve the desired arc, he used quarter-inch plywood, which he soaked in water. He then screwed the plywood to the studs, and repeated the process until he had three layers. (Between each he applied polyurethane glue, which is compatible with damp surfaces.) After installing copper flashings, Roger nailed up the shingles.

Because wood shingles taper from bottom to top, keeping the shingle joints tight and the shingle rows horizontal as they go around the curve required fancy footwork; the shingles must all be especially shaped. Roger tapered the width of the shingles, making the thin tops $\frac{1}{8}$ in. narrower than the thick bottoms. He then trimmed the edges so the width of the backside of the bottom equaled the width of the top. Then the shingles were nailed in place, forming an apparently effortless curve.

EXTERIOR WALLS

All eyes are drawn to the walls of your house first, and it is here you will find the greatest breadth of materials from which to choose. With the vast forests enjoyed by our early American ancestors, wood was often the material used for older houses, with shingles the most common wall cladding.

SHINGLES   From the earliest Colonial times and homes through nearly every style of the golden era, shingles protected American homes.

Many different species of wood were used including pine, white oak, and cedar, but today most shingles are either red or white cedar. Whites, with their rougher surfaces, are used on informal structures like saltboxes or the rear ell of more formal-style homes. When left to weather they turn a beautiful silver gray. The reds, which are smoother, are used on refined styles of homes, such as Shingle or Queen Anne. They are often stained or painted.

CLAPBOARD   Wooden clapboards—long, horizontal boards thin at the top and thick at the bottom—were also common through most styles. Original clapboards are of pine, 3 ft. to 4 ft. long and 6 in. wide with the bottom 4 in. exposed. Originally, where clapboard ends met, carpenters lapped them, creating a scarf to avoid leaky butt seams. Today, the butt joint is quite common and acceptable for your addition because of today's housewraps. Because old growth pine forests have long been depleted and new growth pine is less suitable, western red cedar is the most

common clapboard today. Matching the 4-in. exposure is important—a wider spacing looks less refined and is proportionally incongruous with the existing clapboards.

SHIPLAP AND BOARD AND BATTEN   Shiplap siding and board and batten were used on houses during the golden era, though they were less common than shingles and clapboards. Both are available today, and again, red cedar is most common. Shiplap siding is similar to clapboard in that long boards run horizontally. Shiplap, however, lies flat against the sheathing. Shiplap is found on houses across the country, but it is less common on those built after the revivals of the mid-19th century.

An inexpensive cladding of wide boards placed vertically, board and batten was usually relegated to out buildings like barns and lean-tos—except for Gothic Revival houses. The joint is covered with a wood strip called a batten. Boards and battens were often left rough sawn, reflective of their utilitarian role.

BRICK AND STONE   Both brick and stone are durable and convey timelessness. However, their sheer weight made them a pricey building option unless you had plenty nearby; it was expensive to transport them. Before the railroads were built, houses made from brick or stone were typically near a materials source or connected to it via navigable water. Also, early mortars were composed of lime and sand. While abundant in the southern colonies, limestone deposits were scant in New England. The effect is that most southern Georgian architecture is made of brick while New England houses of that period were usually of wood.

Brick   If the design of your addition calls for new brick to match old, there are three characteristics to consider: color, texture, and uniformity. Until the early

19th century, bricks were made by hand-pressing clay into a mold coated with either sand or water, called sand-struck and water-struck, respectively. Sand-struck bricks have a soft appearance, with sand impregnated in the face. Water-struck bricks have a smooth face, sometimes with a mild sheen, and a richer color. Because bricks of this era were fired at lower temperatures, they have a reddish orange hue, which is one way to date a building.

By the early 19th century, bricks were pressed by machine, which improved their uniformity. By the turn of the 20th century, bricks were made by extruding stiff clay through dies and wire-cutting the extrusion. These bricks are the most uniform. Today, both extruded and molded bricks are produced.

Color is a product of the clay that is used and the firing temperature. Chances are that the clay pits from which your brick was harvested have long been dormant, so consider using locally reclaimed brick of the same era. Many materials, including brick, are salvaged from old buildings before they are demolished.

Stone Stone houses are less common than brick because they were more laborious to build and appropriate stone was often not locally available, particularly along the coast from New Jersey to Texas where most stone is unconsolidated. If you live in an old stone house, the stone was likely quarried nearby.

Like all natural materials, stone, even of the same type, varies in color, veining, and pattern. Stone can be left rough or it can be cut into rectangular shapes called ashlar. The face of ashlar can vary from a smooth sawn face to a rough rock face. Until the 1870s, a more finished stone reflecting greater refinement was popular.

Matching brick is an art. Here the brick and window in the foreground are new but disguised well. Brick and mortar color match, the Flemish bond brick pattern repeats, and the seam between new and old is irregular to mask the juncture.

THE ART OF CRAFT · Stone Walls

When well executed, the facade of a stone house is a work of art: beautiful, permanent, and connected to the land. For this house (as shown on the facing page) the mason, Carl Landis, didn't have to go far to find the right stone: excavating for the addition yielded truckloads of it, which Carl culled for size, color, and texture to match the original wall. To form a right angle at the corners of rubble walls, stones are often dressed, or finished, which is labor intensive. To save costs Carl salvaged dressed stones from a nearby demolished barn.

Before the rubble wall could be built, an acceptable mortar mix matching the color and texture of the original mortar had to be formulated. A lime and sand mix was used, with a small amount of Portland cement to add hardness, and a tint made from a brew of organic compounds to warm the color. The sand was from a local source, always the best way to achieve a match.

Consistent with the original, the wall was laid with flush joints. The mortar joints were dry-brushed just before setting to expose the aggregate that otherwise would take years for the weather to reveal.

Later, Romanesque style, which emphasized the rugged, massive properties of stone, came into vogue. Shingle style and Craftsman style homes frequently featured large boulders.

If you intend to use stone in your addition it is imperative that it matches the original. If no match can be found, clad your addition in a different material to preserve the beauty of the original stone. For example, wooden clapboards are a fine alternative for a new rear ell of a stone house because they are less formal than the stone facades, but still within the general dress code of the house.

Mortar Mortar, which bonds masonry, is another consideration. It varies in profile, joint width, and color. In a freshly laid brick wall mortar joints are shaped by hand, in a procedure called tooling. In any new brickwork, it's important to match the profile of the original mortar joint—anything else can be jarring on historical homes.

If you are using salvaged brick, consider using historical lime mortar. Mortar must be more flexible than brick to allow the bricks to expand and contract. Old

brick moves more because it is softer and more porous than modern brick. Lime mortar is sufficiently elastic to handle the movement but Portland cement is very hard and may crack the brick.

STUCCO AND ADOBE   Stucco is made of the same materials as mortar. Historically, it was applied over adobe, brick, or stone. Today it is usually applied to a wire mesh lath that is stapled to a plywood-sheathed stud wall. The stucco expands around the mesh, holding it in place. Modern stucco, also based on Portland cement, is grayer than the old buff mixes of lime and sand. Stucco is applied in three coats; the topcoat, called the "finish coat," can be textured. As with color, texture should match the original.

THE ROOF

WOOD   Historically, wood shingles were the most common roof material chosen to protect homes from exposure to sun, rain, sleet, hail, and snow. Today, red cedar shingles, when they are installed properly, last 20 to 30 years, longer on a steeply pitched roof, and longer still if oiled or stained. However, some jurisdictions do not permit wood shingle roofs. Talk with your local building department and your home insurance agent before proceeding.

SLATE   Slate makes a wonderful roof; it is beautiful and long-lasting. The first home I owned, an 1874 folk Italianate, has the original slate roof, which is still in good repair after more than 130 years. Vermont, New York, and Pennsylvania were the source of most slate used in the 19th century, and slate is still quarried from this region. Salvaged slate is also available, and can sometimes be a better match because the stone has weathered. Because it is a stone, slate colors and tones vary from black and gray to green or red. Finding a new slate to match the old can be time-consuming, but it's worth the effort. The downside of slate is that it's substantially more expensive than any other roofing. If your home has a slate roof in good shape, keep it; it is an extraordinary asset.

FACING PAGE: The slate on this early 20th-century home looks as good as new, and no substitute material can match its character. **BELOW:** *Red cedar is a good choice for wooden roof shingles. Left to weather, the shingles age to a pleasing blend of grays and browns, and often a longer lifespan than most other species.*

ABOUT THE HOUSE Shingles

Damp shingles are prone to rot, and air is the key to keeping them dry. Old houses were drafty but air moved through the wall and roof cavities and absorbed any moisture trapped behind the shingles. Insulation and vapor barriers changed everything by sealing the cavities. In response, systems had to be developed to lift shingles off the sheathing, creating an air path.

One such product that I use on wooden roofs is an air-circulation membrane, such as Cedar Breather. A loose weave of plastic strands resembling a plate of cooked spaghetti, it is placed on the sheathing and the shingles nailed on top. The irregular pattern of strands ensures a continuous air cavity from eave to ridge vent, keeping your shingles dry and increasing their life span.

METAL   By the end of the 19th century roofs of lead, copper, tin, terne (an alloy of lead and tin), and galvanized iron were common. Before this, roofs of copper or lead were installed, but sparingly. The metal sheets were interlocked for a weather seal. Standing seam roofs, specified for any roof of at least moderate pitch, use long metal sheets that run up and down the roof. The upturned edges are folded and hooked together, creating visually distinctive vertical seams that are narrow and diminutive.

Flat seam roofs, common on shallow-pitched and curvilinear roofs, use smaller metal sheets. Edges are hooked together in a flattened clasp and soldered. Today, all of these metals are available, though tin is rarely used because it deteriorates quickly. The biggest technological changes are in the coatings. Whereas paint protected metal historically, factory-applied coatings are used today.

I often use metal on porch roofs. I prefer copper or lead-coated copper for the color, minimal maintenance, and longevity. Copper and lead oxidize quickly, forming a surface film that protects the metal from further corrosion.

ABOVE LEFT: This old tin roof with diminutive standing seams is painted to lengthen its life. The dormer has a flat seam roof, which covers a brief expanse with ease. **ABOVE RIGHT:** *A new standing-seam metal roof does a good job of emulating the narrow seams of old. Snow guards near the bottom of each bay prevent snow from sliding down onto people and shrubbery below, and deter ice-damming at the eave.*

ABOUT THE HOUSE | Galvanic Action

If you are installing a metal roof you must be attentive to galvanic action, a corrosive reaction between metals of differing electrochemical properties. Whenever dissimilar metals touch in the presence of moisture one of the metals may corrode until it is completely consumed or the electrical contact is broken. I recommend that all metal fasteners, flashings, ridge caps, and any ornamental metal touching a metal roof be made of the identical metal as the metal roof itself.

These new coves are formed by gluing foam blocks of the correct profile to the wall, then skim coating them with joint compound. Coves like these were originally formed using plaster over lath.

THE INTERIOR

Inside your home, you should use materials carefully to tie the old rooms in with the new. But, you also have more design latitude inside. Though it is important to preserve the order of rooms discussed in chapter three, there is opportunity to experiment and indulge your personal tastes.

WALLS   Plaster has been the dominant interior wall finish since Colonial times, and serves as the canvas for a room's further embellishment, from paint or wallpaper to wooden trim or wainscoting. Using a mixture of lime, sand, fiber, and water, a plasterer's skilled hand guided the trowel to build up a smooth, plumb surface, ready for paint, stencil, or wallpaper. Old plaster walls are hard and durable, absorb sound, and are fire resistant. It's a good idea to keep your plaster walls, repairing them rather than replacing them.

Your addition, however, will utilize a technology developed in 1917 that has grown to dominate plastering today: namely, wallboard. Made of compressed gypsum sandwiched between two layers of paper, wallboard dramatically reduces the time needed to finish a house. With "blueboard" and a thin coat of plaster, called

THE ART OF CRAFT   A Spanish Corner

Certain details define a style; for Spanish Revival houses it is rounded plaster corners. To achieve the effect in this house, the doorframe is recessed behind the plaster wall and the plaster curves back to the frame. The craft lies in producing the 1¼ in. corner radius. Contractor Jay Bruder started by attaching gypsum board to the wall framing —a less expensive alternative to blueboard—but he kept it 1¼ in. to the side of the doorframe. Next, he cut a kerf, or notch, in the doorframe. Into the kerf Jay inserted the end of a sheet of metal mesh, to which plaster will hold securely. He then hand-formed the mesh to create the radius and stapled it flush to the gypsum board. Finally, Jay coated the gypsum board with plaster glue and hand-troweled veneer plaster across the wall and around the mesh, stopping at the doorframe. "Cat's faces," subtle irregularities in the plaster, warm the walls with their handmade touch.

veneer plaster, you can combine the efficiency of wallboard with the attractiveness and durability of plaster. And you can match the plaster texture of your original walls.

Plaster corners are an important detail. Before wallboard, plasterers set wood dowels at the corners and plastered to them so outside corners always showed the dowel's curve. Contemporary wallboard construction doesn't need the corner dowel so corners are square. Because a rounded corner is a defining character of old houses, I re-create the rounded corner in the addition. Manufacturers make plastic corners of different radii expressly for veneer plaster construction.

WOODWORK AND FLOORING   Wood is amazing in the myriad roles it fulfills in a room, from the exposed beams supporting the upper floors of a Federal farmhouse to the voluptuously curved window casings in an Italianate to the built-in settee in a Craftsman. When wood is protected from the elements, its rich, organic beauty can be put on display. There are three characteristics to consider when selecting wood: its species, its cut from the log, and its patina.

PLAIN SAWN, QUARTER SAWN, AND RIFT SAWN LUMBER

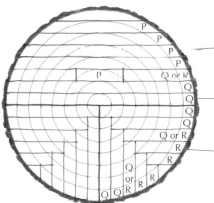

Plain sawn boards have growth rings nearly parallel with the face.

Quarter sawn boards have growth rings at a 60-90 degree angle to the face.

Rift sawn boards have growth rings at a 30-60 degree angle to the face.

The medullar rays are prominent in this quartersawn white oak trim. The underlying grain is tight and vertical.

Grain and color are the two characteristics that most influence which tree species are used in a room. Depending on the period of your home, the most desirable species for natural finishes were white oak, mahogany, or redwood. Walnut, cherry, and fir were also used. When wood was painted, clear pine (free of knots) was historically the most common species. Today, poplar is used for interior painted wood; it is free of knots and has a muted grain that does not show through paint, and it is less expensive than clear pine.

How a board is cut from the log will determine how the grain appears on the board's face, as well as how the board will shrink and expand, and, in some trees, it even determines the color of the wood.

The three ways lumber is cut from a log are plain sawn, rift sawn, and quartersawn (see the diagram on above). Quartersawn lumber has growth rings approximately perpendicular to the board's face. This is a desirable cut for naturally finished wood in formal rooms because it creates highlights, or rays in the grain of certain species such as white oak. Rift sawn has growth rings 30 degrees to 60 degrees to the face yielding tightly spaced parallel lines across the face, called vertical grain. This cut is also popular for formal rooms.

RIGHT: *A hinged door bears stress from hanging off its edge. To minimize warping and racking, carpenters used vertical grain cuts for the stiles and rails, such as in the old pine door. Until roughly the latter part of the 19th century, doors were assembled with mortise and tenon joinery. Look for the telltale tenon end along the door's edge.* **FACING PAGE:** *It will take a while for this new floor to match the 200-hundred-year-old patina of the original, but it is on its way because of good choices. The planks are wide and of random width, and the wood is American walnut resawn from salvaged beams. The small circles are bungs, wooden plugs covering screws.*

On a plain sawn board, the growth rings are roughly parallel to the face of the board and the arc of the growth rings is conspicuous. Plain sawn lumber has an "open grain" face; the grain is irregularly patterned, sometimes forming a V or oval. Plain sawn warps the most. Plain sawn boards are best suited for painted surfaces because the irregular grain when stained or left unpainted visually detracts from the wood's color and a room's formality.

The best way to capture the beauty of old wood is to buy lumber with tight growth rings, cut from the tree in the same manner as is original to the house. This ensures the underlying character of new and old match. Staining the wood can take the curse off the pallor of freshly cut lumber. But be careful not to overdo it; the wood will darken further with age. If you have the time, leave the lumber exposed to sunlight for a while to accelerate the color change. Finally, be patient. Your original boards took time to mature; give your new boards a few years of light and use and they will mellow.

There is a big market for salvaged lumber, usually old beams taken from dismantled buildings. Depending on their age the salvaged beams may be rough sawn or hand hewn. In a post-and-beam house these beams can be used unaltered. Otherwise, they can be re-sawn to the dimension needed. Recut old beams will show some patina. A drawback with salvaged beams is that they will sometimes have nail holes and rust marks from iron fasteners.

FLOORING   Wood again takes top billing as the material of choice. Pine was favored through the early 19th century. The old growth trees yielded hard lumber up to 20 in. wide. As saw mills came online, tongue-and-groove flooring grew in popularity, preferred for its refined appearance: no gaps between boards and no visible nails. It was nailed through the tongue and the nail was hidden in the groove of the next board. White oak and heart pine, either quartersawn or rift sawn, were the popular choices through the early 20th century, with heart pine used in less formal rooms.

Decorative borders of dark woods, such as walnut and ebony, were used in formal rooms of many styles. White oak flooring is still available, though usually

in widths less than 4 in. Heart pine, from the species Longleaf, is hard to find. Companies are now reclaiming Longleaf logs lost long ago in rivers when originally transported by raft. For informal rooms, especially kitchens, bamboo and cork are handsome, and both are harvested in a sustainable manner.

CERAMIC TILE   Tile was rare in American homes before 1870 because it had to be imported from England. By the Victorian period, tile was made in the States and it rapidly grew in popularity for floors, walls, and hearths. The Depression ended tile's rise, mainly because it could be replaced by cheaper synthetic substitutes.

In keeping with the historical precedent, use tile sparingly in houses older than the mid-19th century, typically restricting use to private or informal rooms like the bathroom, kitchen, and mudroom. In baths, honed marble mosaics in simple, Greek-inspired patterns (in keeping with the inspiration for early 19th-century houses) work well. For Victorian and 20th-century revival houses, consider using tile in selected areas as a decorative focal point in a room. I embrace the vivid colors of the era to create showpiece hearths or foyer floors. Today, tile options are numerous and affordable. If your house dates to the peak of decorative ceramic tile production, have some fun with tile in your addition.

HARDWARE AND LIGHTING   Hardware makes the doors, windows, and cabinets in our houses operational. There were many technological advances over the golden era: thumb

FACING PAGE: *Natural materials worked by hand and by time coalesce in restful harmony in this attic bedroom. The window seat beyond and knee wall to the right provide a place to sit and a wall against which to place furniture. They also cleverly hide mechanical ducts that heat the rooms below.*

latches gave way to doorknobs, lock boxes were replaced with mortised locksets, H or H-L hinges succumbed to mortised butt hinges. Windows saw numerous improvements, including the addition of sash locks and lifts and weight-and-chain operation. These advances made it easier and more enjoyable to use the house.

If your house dates before key advancements, it can be difficult to decide whether to match the older technology. If the hardware is prominently associated with the house's era, I encourage its use in your addition, unless its operation will have you pulling your hair out. Thumb latches are one example. They are both visually prominent and strongly associated with Colonial era houses.

Originally, a double-hung window was held open by placing a peg in one of a series of holes underneath the open sash. Newer technologies, such as weight-and-chain or a concealed balance, dramatically improve a window's operation without altering its appearance. I prefer these technologies for most projects.

ABOVE: *New and old merge on this wall. A late-nineteenth century floor grate conceals modern ductwork in the wall. And, an eighteenth century thumb latch handle is teamed with a concealed magnetic catch to open and close the storage door.* RIGHT: *A new dutch door is brought back in time by the salvaged hardware the owners found. The door is hung with strap hinges with driven pintles, and opened with a "German elbow" styled rim lock.* FACING PAGE: *Against a muted backdrop the dark, monochromatic tile of this fireplace surround draws attention without being overbearing. Modest tile accents give the surround a hand-crafted feel.*

Hardware, particularly doorknobs and rosettes, commonly reinforces the order of rooms from public to private. Brass, bronze, or nickel-plated doorknobs might be used in formal rooms while mercury knobs were used in private rooms. I continue this tradition in an addition. If specifying a metal doorknob and rosette, I don't recommend a lacquer coating, which preserves the metal in an artificially bright finish. Many contemporary latchsets—the mechanical portion of the door latch—require that a large hole be bored in the door face. Avoid these latches because they force the use of a wide rosette, out of balance with its accompanying knob. Instead, team up your diminutive rosette with a small-bored tubular latch.

Light fixtures—sconces, chandeliers, and pendants—whether oil, gas, or electric have long been the domain of artisans. New fixtures are acceptable, but study the craftsmanship before you make your purchase. There is a near endless range of options, so allow time to visit several showrooms and Web sites. Another

FACING PAGE: *Original lighting was so fragile that to find it intact and in good working order is a rarity. Here, a delicately ornamented piece fits right in with its Spanish Colonial Revival setting.*
RIGHT: *This salvaged sconce, converted to electricity, brings old world artisanship to the addition of this home.*
BELOW LEFT: *Light fixtures should be decorative. This new fixture illuminates the family entry, and the handcrafted twists and turns in the metal add flair.*
BELOW RIGHT: *This porcelain knob is simple, appropriate for the attic bedroom where it is located. The rosette is unlaquered brass and in balance with the knob.*

An iron strap hinge holds an old beadboard door worn from years of use. An adjacent closet has a salvaged thumb latch in the spade style. Both are eighteenth century technology.

THE ART OF CRAFT   Shaping a Fireplace

Architect James McCrery, following the model of Colonial-era summer kitchen fireplaces, came up with a straightforward design for this Virginia fireplace (shown in photo at left). He first sized the firebox, making it as large as permitted today. (To ensure proper draft, building codes require that flue size and chimney height increase with the size of the firebox.) Because the addition was one story, chimney height was the limiting factor, as a tall chimney would be out of balance

Choosing the right brick was foremost. Colonial era bricks were handmade, irregularly sized, with minor facial blemishes and color variation. Capturing the handcraft of the period is important, so James used brick salvaged from two Colonial era buildings. These were culled for quality, hand-cleaned, and laid in a running bond pattern.

Both the fireplace legs and the hearth are made of reclaimed Virginia sandstone, which complements the brick in color, finish, and is durable. Spanning the opening is a large wood lintel, salvaged from an 18th-century fireplace. The back had been scorched giving some fire resistance. The back and underside were covered with copper sheet for further protection. (Before incorporating this detail in your addition, check with your building department for compliance.) The inside of the firebox is modern firebrick, which is quickly being disguised by the soot of frequent use.

option is to use salvaged lighting fixtures, especially if your house predates electricity. There are shops that specialize in converting oil, gas, and candle fixtures to electrical operation. If you are ambitious, rummage through antique sales for the perfect fixture, and then ask an electrician to wire it. Be sure the electrician is experienced in this work, and always make sure any rewired fixture meets UL requirements to ensure its safe operation.

CABINETRY   Built-in cabinets, such as hutches, butler pantries, and bookshelves, were popular throughout the golden era. These old cabinets remain popular today. Cabinets were typically woven into the room's design, sharing trim and carrying through key regulating lines. In contemporary home construction, built-in cabinets have been all but eliminated.

As they have little historical precedent, both kitchen and bathroom cabinetry have more leeway for design exploration. The master bath vanity, in particular, can be an objet d'art, a jewel tucked away just for you. Stay within the vocabulary of the style, but use an unusual species of wood and cap it boldly with a statement-making stone counter. Kitchen cabinets require more restraint, because they are expansive and usually open to other rooms. For a little spice, introduce a counter with attitude: cast-in-place concrete, stainless steel, or walnut butcher block. A thick slab of soapstone, honed and oiled, can be equally dramatic. Keep in mind that different materials have different qualities, positive and negative. Review them carefully before selecting an uncommon counter material.

FIREPLACES   The fireplace is the focal point of any room. Give it special attention in your addition. The masonry surrounding the firebox was most often brick through the Federal style. The brick of the period is as warm as the fire it surrounds, from the hand-molded individuality to the orange hue. Such brick is hard to match with new brick; I recommend reclaimed brick. Few brick are needed for the firebox surround, so one solution I have used is to remove a few brick from a hidden portion of an original chimney, replace them with new brick, and use the old brick for my new fireplace.

By the Victorian era, the firebox surround became a way to display an exotic material, including rubble stone, honed marble, and glazed tile or brick. Twentieth-century styles continued the diversified palette, though less flamboyantly. I encourage you to install a special material in your new Victorian-era fireplace; it would be in the spirit of the house, and is another way to personalize your design. The hearth employs a similar array of materials. Though the surround and hearth need not match, they should be made from the same family of materials and given a similar finish.

NEW OLD MATERIALS

Are substitution materials necessary? Yes, but you should turn to them only as a last resort. Natural materials have longevity. When you encounter premature deterioration of a natural material, it is usually an inferior grade or installed improperly. For example, not long before my wife and I purchased our home, a carpenter had replaced a section of wooden balustrade on the front porch. Unfortunately, he

ABOVE: *This shed roof addition that is the home's new kitchen embraces the breadth of materials available today. Taking its cues from the galvanized corrugated metal roofs that dominated the Bay Area when the original shed was built, a sheet of translucent Kalwall® rests upon the exposed rafters and brightens the space below with diffuse light.* LEFT: *This new fireplace in an early twentieth century home is subdued, appropriate for the period. The surround is an ashlar rubble, matching the original stone of the house's foundation.*

used poplar, which is wonderful for interior trim, but outside it rots at the mere threat of rain. When we moved in it had already been removed and tossed in the basement. Had the carpenter used the heartwood of cedar, a rot-resistant species, the balustrade today would need nothing more than a coat of paint.

I consider using substitute materials in two circumstances: when the cost of using the original material is prohibitive and when the original material does not meet the requirements of current building codes. Written to protect the health, safety, and welfare of the public, they sometimes affect your choice of materials. An example mentioned earlier is a wood shingle roof, now banned in some locales. In earthquake zones, code restrictions also govern the use of masonry.

SOMETIMES NEW WILL DO   Cementitious board, a composite that includes cellulose fibers, is one of the few viable substitutes for wooden clapboard. The untextured boards appear similar, and they are thermally stable and not vulnerable to moisture. Also, paint adheres to cementitious boards longer than it does to wood boards.

Asphalt composition shingles have been used for nearly 100 years, and they are the dominant roofing material today. They are so different from the 19th-century roofscapes of wooden shingles, slate, and clay tiles that I don't consider asphalt shingles a substitution, but an alternative. The three-tab shingle is the quintessential asphalt shingle, and I prefer it for its simplicity. It can be a cost-effective option for a rear ell out of public view.

Synthetic slate is a promising new product. It is polymer-based, mold-formed, and contains recycled rubber. Though less expensive than true slate, it is costly. Manufacturers have done a good job at capturing the texture of slate, and they provide shingles of different shapes to simulate the random cleft. So far, however, I've not seen a product with the natural color variation of true slate, and synthetic slate roofs look unnaturally homogenous. Because the product is only about a decade old, I am also concerned about its ability to keep its color and to not become brittle.

The natural materials of your home are key to its allure. Synthetic substitutes, with few exceptions, fail to evoke a visceral response–there's no plucking of the heartstrings.

TOP: *Because building codes disallow masonry chimneys in the Los Angeles area, the new chimney in the foreground is a metal flue enclosed by stucco-covered steel studs. It resides comfortably next to the original masonry fireplace.*
LEFT: *Asphalt shingles were common on homes in the 20th century, such as this Cape Cod revival. The three-tab shingle is simple and understated, and is appropriate for the house.* **BOTTOM:** *The mansard roof of this Second Empire home is covered in synthetic slate—a good choice for this style of house.*

243

PLAYING BY THE RULES

Tudor Revival · Bronxville, New York

L ooks can be deceiving. Behind a facade of bold shapes and hefty materials, this Tudor Revival house was only a modest collection of rooms. Informal rooms were either small or nonexistent. There was no family room, and the kitchen was cramped and remote. The owners enjoy cooking and they wanted a spacious kitchen. Next to the kitchen, they wanted an informal room where family could dine casually and guests could relax while meals were prepared. The second floor was uncomfortably tight; the stair, two bedrooms, and an outdated bath opened onto a 4-ft. hall. A room sized for a nursery had been pressed into service as a bedroom. A successful addition would relieve these problems.

The owners liked the strong character of their Tudor style exterior and wanted to preserve it. The front entry is well-composed and deftly uses materials and forms of the style. A steeply sloped gable rises over the white oak entry door. The second story is half timbered and cantilevered over the entry, a nod to the English medieval architecture in which the style is rooted. A large chimney of rubble stone and brick stakes the house firmly to the ground. To either side of the entry short wings sit back from the front gable. Both wings are less detailed than the entry gable, giving it substantial prominence.

The original house is seen front and center, the massive chimney its center of gravity. Receding from view to the right is the addition, which uses the same materials as the formal facade, but in a less dramatic way.

ABOVE: *Unusual materials make the new kitchen fun to be in, and simple details keep the room from overstepping its role in the house. White oak, a favored material of the style, finishes the kitchen in amber. Hand-painted tiles of the Tuscan countryside are substituted for stainless steel above the range. A broad cased opening marks the kitchen's boundary.* RIGHT: *A new balustrade next to the family room has simple details and is left natural to accentuate the materials and their joinery.* FAR RIGHT: *The house before the addition.* FACING PAGE (FLOOR PLAN): *The kitchen is accessed through a butler's pantry portal, and shielded from the foyer and living room. A simple, efficient, and open plan replaces the zigzag halls and odd room locations.*

BEFORE

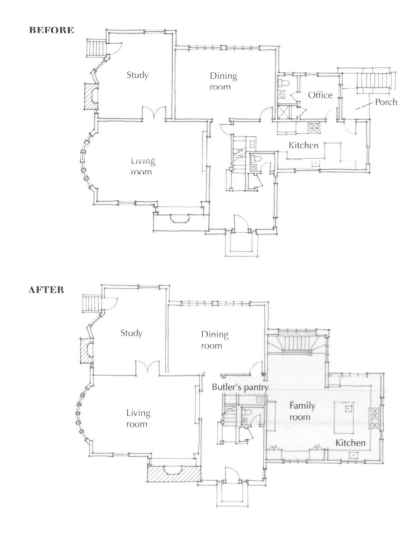

Study

Dining room

Office

Porch

Kitchen

Living room

AFTER

Study

Dining room

Butler's pantry

Family room

Living room

Kitchen

Tudor Revival (1890–1940)

During America's time of period revivals many people built homes reminiscent of late-medieval English cottage and manor houses. Different revival styles drew on differing characteristics for inspiration. For Tudor Revival, the plaster-coated materials and framing were most influential. Though called Tudor Revival, this style is usually a mixture of the English styles of the 16th and early 17th centuries: Tudor, Elizabethan, and Jacobean. Many Tudor Revival homes are easily recognized by their false half timber facades. Originally, these timbers were the house's structural frame, infilled with clay and brick, but in Revival homes they are decorative. Contemporaneous with Arts and Crafts, Tudor Revival homes also eschew manufactured products for those handmade. Houses have less ornament, with greater attention to materials and their joinery.

Tudor houses are usually imposing, with steeply pitched, cross-gabled slate roofs, and massive chimneys often placed next to the entry. Facades use a combination of stone, patterned brick, and half timbering with plaster. Windows are narrow casement, with small panes of leaded glass, sometimes diamond shaped. Hardware and light fixtures are of wrought iron. By the 1930s, the style became part of the American vernacular.

PRESERVING CHARACTER

Because the rooms of the addition are informal, it is placed to the right of the front entry, away from the formal rooms on the left. The addition envelops the old wing and follows its shape with a tall cross-gable and shed dormers. The new wing appears nearly identical to the old, but it is 7 ft. longer and the front facade is set 8 ft. closer to the main facade. Though these changes are significant, key principles of the house were respected and its character preserved. For example, the new wing's ridge does not rise higher than the main ridge. Also, the wing's facade is still set 5 ft. back from the main facade. Finally, the eave line of the addition is set lower than that of the original house.

In the extended wing there are two shed dormers rather than one as in the original wing. This maintains the wing's balance, as a single dormer would have left a long expanse of roof and wall.

BELOW: *Built-in cabinets can be more than storage bins. Here the built-in shelves and cabinets create a wonderful window seat in the new bedroom. The arch is inspired by the arched cased opening that defines the end of the stair hall.*

FACING PAGE: *The procession of formal rooms is preserved by placing the addition out of its path. But the kitchen is closer than ever, just a quick turn to the right before the end of the hall.*

Departing from the original, the new shed dormers cantilever past the first floor and are finished with half timbering, previously reserved for the entry. This modest change is what makes the addition so successful. The cantilever and half timbering spare the wing's facade from banality, but by limiting these borrowed features to the dormers, the addition does not steal the show from the entry.

A MATERIAL INVERSION

Naturally finished wood in homes of this era is normally more formal than painted wood. It may seem odd then that the new kitchen and family room are naturally finished white oak, while the wood elsewhere is painted. This inversion highlights the kitchen, a room special to the owners. But the design of the cabinets relaxes the room and gives it an informal air. The cabinets are simple, with no moldings except a small crown. By contrast, the built-in cabinets in the living room have raised panels with moldings, and the crown molding is taller and more complex in shape. The choice of hardware also reinforces the room roles. The kitchen uses bin pulls, historically used in such places as butler pantries, while the living room uses delicately proportioned brass knobs. And, to remind us that in this house painted wood reigns, the kitchen centerpiece island is painted and more finely detailed than the oak cabinets. Together these design decisions allow for personal expression in a room without historical precedent, while keeping the kitchen grounded in the overall order of rooms.

Upstairs the new bedroom and bath adhere to precedent; both are painted wood and plaster. The bedroom has a built-in cabinet and window seat of painted beadboard and cabinetry of understated design.

A quick look at the "before" and "after" photos may leave you thinking nothing changed. That is precisely why this is such a successful addition. The floor plan grew modestly, but out of it arose rooms suited for today's lifestyle and better circulation making the house more enjoyable and accessible. For most of us living in old houses, this is all we need.

HOLDING TIME STILL

Colonial · Alexandria, Virginia

In Joe Reeder's 1772 home time seems to have stood still. The original two-room house was built by a farmer on land outside of Alexandria, Virginia. Behind the house, a brick structure served as a summer kitchen and a place to conduct business. Over the next 35 years the house grew and the summer kitchen was incorporated into the floor plan. Then nearly 200 years passed with little change. When Joe bought the house, only its fourth owner, the privies were still standing (though not in use), and the summer kitchen was still functional. Joe is a collector of early Americana and prized the house for its history, but he wanted to make it more livable. He wanted a new kitchen and an updated bath.

Alexandria has grown around the farmhouse over the years and the house is now within the historic district. As it is one of the oldest houses in the district, a design that put the character of the old house first was paramount.

The new kitchen is a blend of old and new. The materials and their assembly are of the house's era and firmly ground the room in tradition. A cathedral ceiling and strong connection to the outdoors make the room enjoyable today.

A DELICATE DECISION

The house sits on a corner and is very visible. To preserve the public views, architect James McCrery designed the addition on a sliver of land behind the house, against the property line. There it would be hidden from public view, but it did require yet another round of town approvals, this time for a zoning variance.

James and Joe worked like a surgical team placing the addition. It meets the original house along only one wall and joins it via a pre-existing door; no new openings were required. The foundation supporting the new walls stands clear of the old house to ensure the old walls are not undermined. If the house is someday given to the town as a museum, the addition could be easily removed without damage to the historical structure.

AN IDENTITY OF ITS OWN

The new kitchen is modest at just 160 sq. ft., but dramatic. It has a cathedral ceiling, a prominent cooking fireplace, and a pair of Dutch doors leading outside that are wide enough for a Model T. The room is a counterpoint to the plainspoken

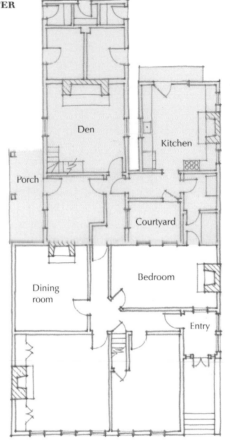

Den

Kitchen

Porch

Courtyard

Dining room

Bedroom

Entry

RIGHT: *The story of the house's piecemeal growth is evident in the floor plan, a collection of casually organized rooms. For the owner, the addition had to preserve the house's story and add a new chapter. The addition, placed alongside but not attached to the old ell, preserves the old wall. New and old meet briefly, where a pre-existing door opens into the kitchen hall.* **FACING PAGE LEFT:** *A place for refuse is now a place of refuge. This once neglected yard is now the site of a vibrant kitchen.* **FACING PAGE RIGHT:** *In the 1790s, the front entry was moved to the side to make way for a wider street. Since then the front facade is unchanged, as is true with much of the rest of the house. The architect's respectful placement of the new kitchen wing ensures this historical facade will live on.*

character of the original. Yet the materials work to tie it to the old house. The floors are walnut planks of random width sawn from salvaged beams. Concessions made to the floor's heavy use include bungs—wood plugs flush with the floor that cover nails—and a matte coat of polyurethane. The walls are post and beam construction of salvaged oak, left exposed. The ceiling rafters are also salvaged, their rough-sawn faces still visible, and assembled by methods common to the period, including half-lapped joinery and friction-fit dowels. Over the rafters run wide planks, called board sheathing, onto which the roof material is attached. Planks are no longer used for sheathing today, but they are essential to the ambience of this kitchen.

Anchoring the lofty kitchen is a cooking fireplace complete with an iron crane. Made from reclaimed stone and brick, the fireplace assumes its historical role as the center of family life. Opposite is an eclectic collection of antique dry sinks, aligned and covered with a butcher block counter. Two more antiques complete the cabinet storage: a wall-mounted china cabinet and large hutch that serves as a

RIGHT: *This new kitchen window looks across into the original summer kitchen. The window was made by a local craftsman trained in traditional window making. It matches the old windows in size and proportion.* BELOW: *The kitchen ceiling is a union of natural materials and handcraft. Reclaimed white oak timbers are joined with pegged lap joints. The pegs were forced by sledgehammer through a crimper plate that temporarily reduces their diameter, then soaked in water and driven through predrilled holes. They will hold fast for generations.* FACING PAGE: *Viewed from the private oasis of the patio, the new kitchen is filled with early Americana and awash in old world charm. To the right, the addition stops inches short of the old brick summer kitchen, leaving intact its architectural history for future generations.*

pantry. The cabinets are rich in character from age and use and feel like an extension of the aged walls and floors.

At the end of this dynamic room are the Dutch doors, made of mahogany and finished to a low luster, but simply detailed. The upper leaves have 12 glass panes for ample light and a strong connection to the outdoors, another nod to our lifestyle today.

SOUTHERN HOSPITALITY

At the end of our photo shoot, Joe invited several of our team to join him for food and drink in his new kitchen. Relaxing in a chair almost as old as the house, and with food preparations swirling about me, I realized what a success this modest addition is. I felt that I was in an old house; the careful choice of materials, finishes, and assembly are a natural extension of the 18th-century home. Yet I was enjoying the kitchen's contemporary features. The Dutch doors were thrown back so that a soft breeze and afternoon light flowed through the expansive opening. And the efficiency of smartly organized modern appliances allowed hors d'oeuvres to be served before we drank our toast.

REVIVING A RETREAT

Carpenter Gothic · Cape Cod, Massachusetts

At 350 sq. ft., this summerhouse was smaller than some master bedroom suites. Nonetheless, owner and architect Jane Treacy happily spent many summers here with her family. They loved the house's history and its straightforward construction harkening back to a simpler time. Naturally, amenities were few: a kitchen sink, a small range, and a toilet and shower reached by going outside. The one bedroom could only accommodate a floor mattress.

Jane wanted a full bedroom, a bath, and a kitchen sized for daily use, including a small eating area. This would be a modest addition for most houses, but it would more than double Jane's house. Preserving scale and style were essential, as was maintaining simplicity.

HUMBLE ROOTS

In the mid-19th century Methodists organized a retreat at this site. Families initially gathered under tents but as they returned annually to the same plot their tents gave way to houses. Restrained by their tiny plots, the houses are unusually petite. Jane's house is Carpenter Gothic, a folk version of Gothic Revival. It is simply constructed of wood. Outside, vertical tongue-and-groove boards cover the stud walls accentuating the height of the house. Inside, both wall and ceiling framing are bare. The house is neither insulated nor heated.

The addition is larger than the 1880 cottage it sits behind. Yet, by matching materials, trim, color, and roof shape, it blends with the cottage. Keeping the new eave low and opening the new first floor walls for a screened porch makes the addition less imposing.

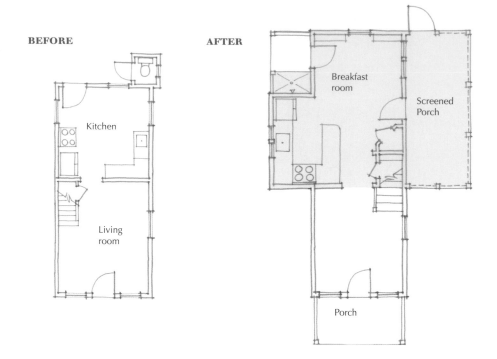

BEFORE   AFTER

Kitchen

Living room

Breakfast room

Screened Porch

Porch

PRESERVING THE JEWEL

The original cottage is untouched. The addition is placed behind it. Though larger, the addition is held in check by keeping the new roof low, matching the original roof slope, aligning the eaves, and using dormers to capture critical headroom. Outside, the addition uses the same materials, of the same dimension, as the original. Walls, rafter tails, rake boards, and window casings all match. Proportions were carefully followed, too. The windows are tall and the roof is steep, both Gothic trademarks. New gable dormers are sized to match the original gable roof. The addition, made from the same DNA, appears to be nudging the original house forward to center stage and serves as the setting for the original jewel.

Inside, the addition is faithful to the precedent of the historical house: unadorned, without even the most basic finishes. The wall and floor framing are unabashedly exposed. The spruce pine framing is of construction grade lumber with visible knots, reinforcing the humble character of the house. The new windows are wood, single-glazed, with razor thin muntins like the originals. The kitchen cabinets, plain and utilitarian, were salvaged from a mid-20th-century house and covered with a plastic laminate counter. Frugal and functional, this decision, too, reinforces the aesthetic of the house.

As a finishing touch, Jane washed the walls and cabinets in white, quieting their irregular faces. The ceiling and windows are left natural for a color accent, and the floor is painted in bright hues to warm the still unheated house when the sea breeze is cold. Because of Jane's sensitivity to the former campground cottage, her summerhouse will remain an alluring retreat for years to come.

FACING PAGE. *With a push here and a nudge there, the new floor plan makes this summer retreat more livable. Removed from the flow of traffic, the new kitchen has more prep and storage area. The only alteration to the original cottage is a new stair that replaces one too steep and narrow.* LEFT: *The original bedroom reminds contemporary retreaters of the site's origin as a campground for tents.* BOTTOM LEFT: *The original living room looks onto the communal area of the campground. It is unchanged except for a more comfortable stair, seen in the foreground. The bare bones honesty of the room continues in the addition.* BOTTOM RIGHT: *Size is relative. Only 10 ft. wide and 9 ft. deep, the new breakfast area would be out of scale in many homes, but is perfect in this delicate cottage.*

A HOME BUILT FROM THE LAND

Federal · Reading, Pennsylvania

This 1829 farmhouse in the rolling hills of eastern Pennsylvania is crafted from the materials that surround it: fieldstone, pine, and oak. The patient hands of time have turned the pine floors amber and the stone walls a color wheel of earth tones. The house is one with the land and history, which is precisely why the owners, two refugees from Manhattan, bought it.

The house Jeff Gorrin and Susan Fetterolf found was small: three rooms on the first floor, a kitchen the size of a pantry, and three bedrooms upstairs. One bathroom served the entire house. They needed a library to hold their book collection, a contemporary kitchen, a family room more intimate than the original parlors, a home office, and a master suite. They entrusted architects Peter Zimmerman and John Toates to find a solution that balanced their practical needs with their aesthetic sensibilities.

MAKING NEW FROM OLD

The first decision Jeff and Susan made was to use natural materials, especially salvaged materials of the era. All of the timbers for the addition were taken from one 18th-century house. As in the original house, ceilings are framed of exposed oak timbers, some as big as 8 in. by 11 in. Other than being cut to length the old timbers are unaltered, preserving their darkened faces and axe and saw markings. Roof sheathing and sub-flooring, commonly of plywood today, were made of reclaimed pine boards because their surfaces are visible in the unfinished ceiling.

The summer kitchen, nearly 200 years old and going strong, needs only an occasional tune-up. The wood needs to be painted every 10 years, the mortar repointed every 50 years. The clay roof tiles and stone walls still have many years of life in them.

For Jeff and Susan the hardware was a defining element of the house. Though period hardware lacked technological conveniences of later eras, keeping the materials and craftsmanship intact was more important than convenience. For the new single-hung windows made of white oak, a wooden peg secures the lower sash when closed and a prop stick holds it open. Doors hang with iron strap, H or HL hinges, and they open with thumb latches; exterior doors have surface-mounted rim locks.

Finding all this early 19th-century hardware was an adventure. One expedition became many as they traveled as far as northern New England. Once their collection was complete, they sorted it according to style and formality and installed it in rooms of comparable formality. Their hard work was worth it. Every room is a gallery for a different blacksmith's craft, but the collection remains unified.

Susan and Jeff applied similar rigor to areas of the house that had no historical precedent. The mudroom, powder room, and family bath are furnished with found

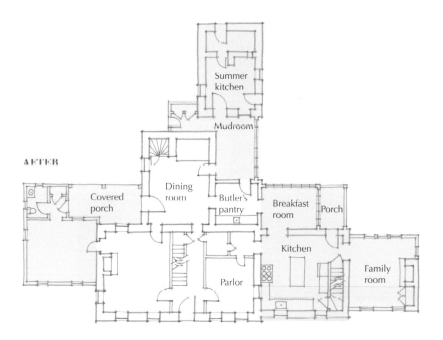

AFTER

Summer kitchen

Mudroom

Dining room

Butler's pantry

Breakfast room

Porch

Covered porch

Kitchen

Parlor

Family room

LEFT: *The addition is spread around three sides of the stone house. To the left a library is added and it opens to the parlor, appropriate for two formal rooms. The right side is the casual wing of the house, with limited connection to the parlor. Support rooms and farmer's porches are to the rear and removed from the formal side of the house.* **ABOVE:** *The architects worked to preserve the formality of the front facade. The original house stands forward of, and taller than, the additions on either side; and the eaves, or gutter lines, of both new wings are lower than the original eave.* **FACING PAGE LEFT:** *This is a view of the back of the house before the addition. The original house and summer kitchen are separated by a connector. The architects worked carefully to preserve this relationship in their addition.* **FACING PAGE RIGHT:** *Buildings crafted of natural materials are timeless. Suspend time in your addition by using natural materials. Select the materials to be in harmony with your original house and you will leave an enduring legacy for future generations to enjoy.*

objects. They purchased antique cabinets for the vanities and antique vessels for the washbowls. Drains and waterlines were added. New faucets match the antiques in style and they are finished in unlacquered brass oxidized to a dark brown.

THE KITCHEN COLLAGE

The kitchen is a symphony of materials orchestrated into a beautiful room. It, too, uses reclaimed materials: random width unfinished beadboard on the walls and waxed plank floors. This leaves the patina in place and reinforces the informality of the room. The cabinets are new but not of uniform design, like a collage. It is a clever arrangement that makes the room feel smaller, so that it doesn't overpower the older, smaller rooms nearby.

KEEPING IT MODEST

The old farmhouse was small and simply detailed, but proudly crafted. Preserving the scale, craft, and charm was paramount. Because the addition was to be as large as the original house the architects divided it into three sections, placing one on each side of the house and one in the rear. The new wings to either side are telescopes. The balance and formality of the front facade is preserved. The rear addition is sheltered by an assortment of gable and shed roofs casually organized as one would expect on the rear of an old farmhouse. The addition also connects with the old summer kitchen, adding "reclaimed" floor area to the house.

The stone facade is the first thing you notice upon arriving at the house. Its warmth and permanence leave a lasting impression. The architects used stone sparingly in the addition so as not to steal the stage from the original. The wing

ABOVE: *The new family room has a cathedral ceiling, rare in early 19th-century rooms. Here it works well because antique materials and framing methods are used. Also, the ceiling joists, horizontal boards that "tie" opposing sides of a roof together, give the room a human scale and suggest that a plaster ceiling may have once hung from them.*

to the right of the front facade telescopes in two sections. The first section, which is two stories, is stone taken from the yard and laid to match the original. The second section, one-story tall, is clapboard except for the chimney end wall. All other new wings are clapboard, the most formal of wood sidings but less formal than stone, distinguishing them from the original house. Clapboards and trim are painted olive green, giving the facades a monolithic appearance that also helps them recede from prominence. To the rear, the addition is low slung and covered with a standing seam metal roof painted red oxide to blend with the red clay tiles of the summer kitchen. Casement windows, hidden from public view, wrap the walls to take in the private garden and bucolic setting.

Jeff and Susan preserved the spirit of a fine home built when homes were of necessity made from their surroundings and were a part of the land. They built for future generations as well as themselves, and they have added greatly to the joy that may be had in this house.

ABOVE: *The new kitchen is large enough to host a party. The owners shunned a uniform kitchen in favor of a collection of materials deftly organized. A pewter counter caps the island and Italian marble of a similar gray finishes the perimeter cabinets. Two porcelain farmer's sinks paired with brushed nickel spigots stand ready to wash or fill anything coming their way.* NEXT SPREAD: *The back addition is informal. Windows and doors are placed where needed without regard to formal aesthetic rules. Shed dormers, a less formal roof shape, cover the lower parts of the house while gables cap the taller portions beyond.*

FEATURE HOUSES REFERENCE LIST

A HOME ON THE HUDSON (P. 44)
Radoslav Opacic AIA Architects
24 North Astor
Irvington, NY 10533
(914) 591-4306
www.opacicarchitects.com
Builder: Chilmark Builders, Inc.
Pleasantville, NY

SAVING BEAUTY (P. 52)
Design Associates, Inc.
432 Columbia Street
Cambridge, MA 02141
(617) 661-9082
www.design-associates.com
Frank Shirley, Project Manager
Builder: Charron Construction
Danvers, MA

BALANCING INSIDE AND OUT (P. 60)
Kevin Oreck Architect
113-1/2 North La Brea Avenue,
Suite 114
Los Angeles, CA 90036
(323) 692-0896
www.kevinoreckarchitect.com
Builder: Bruder Construction
Bell Canyon, CA

BEAUTY IS IN THE DETAILS (P. 68)
Eck | MacNeely Architects
560 Harrison Avenue, Suite 403
Boston, MA 02118
(617) 367-9696
www.eckmacneely.com
Design Consultant: Phil Duffy
Builder: G F Rhode Construction
Boston, MA

FOURSQUARE AND MANY YEARS AGO (P. 108)
Cunningham + Quill Architects, PLLC
1054 31st Street NW, Suite 315
Washington, DC 20007
(202) 337-0090
www.cunninghamquill.com
Builder: Acadia Contractors,
Bethesda, MD

EMBRACING A BOLD IDEA (P. 114)
Peter Zimmerman Architects
828 Old Lancaster Road
Berwyn, PA 19312
(610) 647-6970
www.pzarchitects.com
Builder: Restore 'N More, Inc.
Manheim, PA

FROM CHAOTIC TO CASUAL AND COMFORTABLE (P. 122)
Treacy & Eagleburger Architects, PC
3335 Connecticut Avenue NW, 2nd Floor
Washington, DC 20008
(202) 362-5226
www.treacyeagleburger.com
Builder: Carson & Associates
Washington, DC

A BAY AREA BEAUTY (P. 128)
David S. Gast & Associates
1746 Union Street
San Francisco, CA 94123
(415) 885-2946
www.gastarchitects.com

A WELL-CRAFTED DREAM (P. 168)
Carr, Lynch & Sandell, Inc.
1385 Cambridge Street
Cambridge, MA 02139
(617) 661-6566
www.carrlynchsandell.com
Builder: St. Onge Building & Renovations
Scituate, MA

BREATHING ROOM (P. 174)

Richard Bergmann Architects
63 Park Street
New Canaan, CT 06840
(203) 966-9505
Interior Design: Christine Fleischi, Enticements
New Canaan, CT

A VICTORIAN WITH HUMILITY (P. 180)

Albert, Righter, and Tittmann Architects, Inc.
8 Winter Street
Boston, MA 02108
(617) 451-5740
www.alriti.com
Builder: Ed Howland
Sherborn, MA

MAKING BIG THINGS LOOK SMALL (P. 186)

Frank Shirley Architects
75 Henry Street
Cambridge, MA 02139
(617) 547-3355
www.frankshirleyarchitects.com

A BELOVED TREASURE GLITTERS IN THE SUN (P. 190)

Turnbull Griffin Haesloop Architects
1660 Bush Street, Suite 200
San Francisco, CA 94109
(415) 441-2300
www.tgharchitects.com

PLAYING BY THE RULES (P. 256)

Radoslav Opacic AIA Architects
24 North Astor
Irvington, NY 10533
(914) 591-4306
www.opacicarchitects.com
Builder: Jack Dos Santos Home Improvements
Yonkers, NY

HOLDING TIME STILL (P. 242)

Franck Lohsen McCrery, Architects
1715 N. Street NW
Washington, DC 20036
(202) 223-9449
www.flmarchitects.com

REVIVING A RETREAT (P. 248)

Treacy & Eagleburger Architects, PC
3335 Connecticut Avenue NW, 2nd Floor
Washington, DC 20008
(202) 362-5226
www.treacyeagleburger.com
Builder: Philbrook Engineering
Dennis, MA

A HOME BUILT FROM THE LAND (P. 252)

Peter Zimmerman Architects
828 Old Lancaster Road
Berwyn, PA 19312
(610) 647-6970
www.pzarchitects.com
Builder: Griffiths Construction, Inc.
Chester Springs, PA

To get more information about your old house and the resources available, contact the National Trust for Historic Preservation (www.nthp.org) and/or the National Register of Historic Places (www.cr.nps.gov/nr), where you can also learn more about the Secretary of the Interior's Standards for the preservation of historic buildings.

GLOSSARY

A

ALIGNMENT LINE: a regulating line used to align the edges of architectural elements.

ARCADE: a series of arches supported by columns.

ARCHITRAVE: in classical architecture, the lowest of the three main parts of an entablature, the beam that rests upon the columns.

ARTS AND CRAFTS: an aesthetic movement (1870–1920) dedicated to reestablishing the importance of craftsmanship; began in England and spread to the United States, where it flourished in the West producing designs that were American originals; looked to nature rather than history for inspiration, featured local materials, natural woods, joinery, low slung roofs, deep front porches, dramatic overhangs, and masculine columns.

ASHLAR: a rectangular block of hewn stone used in building.

B

BACKBAND: a piece of trim applied around the perimeter of casings, usually to enhance the casing's formality.

BALLOON FRAMING: a system of wood-frame construction in which the studs are continuous from the foundation sill to the top wall plate, held together entirely by nails; made possible in the 19th century by the availability of lumber sawed to uniform sizes; replaced slower post-and-beam construction using less-skilled labor and yet produced buildings that were stronger and more apt to be square and plumb.

BALUSTER: the thin, narrow support of a railing often turned on a lathe to an intricate shape.

BALUSTRADE: a series of balusters and the railing they support.

BANQUETTE: a built-in bench, especially along a wall.

BASE: the molded foot of a column or pilaster.

BASEBOARD: finish trim along the bottom of a wall the height of which influences a room's formality.

BAY WINDOW: a windowed projection from an outside wall, three sided in plan.

BELLY CASING: profiled trim that is symmetrical in section with the middle portion convex; it can be either formal or informal.

BLUE BOARD: sheetrock that has been coated to prevent the absorption of moisture; used for veneer plaster finishes.

BOARD AND BATTEN: a siding system in which the seams between wide vertical boards are covered by narrow boards, both usually rough sawn.

BOW WINDOW: a windowed projection from an outside wall, curved in plan.

BRACKET: a projection providing support, either structural or visual, under cornices, balconies, and other overhanging members.

BROKEN PEDIMENT: a pediment interrupted at the apex by an opening that highlights a carved detail, frequently an urn.

BUNGALOW: a small one- or 1½-story dwelling with a low-pitched roof, often with a prominent front veranda; popular in Southern California at the turn of the 20th century, the most popular were of the Craftsman style, which emerged from the Arts-and-Crafts movement.

BUTT JOINT: a simple joint formed by joining the squared ends of two boards.

C

CANTILEVER: a portion of a facade, often an upper floor, that projects beyond the facade below.

CAPE COD: a symmetrical 1½-story rectangular frame house with a steep shingle roof having side gables, little overhang, and no dormers; sides covered by shingles, little ornamentation; multipaned double hung windows with shutters; chimney and front door on the centerline.

CAPITAL: the decorative head of a column or pilaster crowning the shaft and supporting the entablature, with decoration varying according to architectural style.

CASED OPENING: an opening finished with doorjambs and trim, but without a door; used for transitions.

CASEMENT: a window with the sash hung vertically, hinged at the side, and opening inward or outward.

CASING: a flat, decorative molding that covers the inside edge of window and door jambs and the rough openings between the jamb and the wall.

CATHEDRAL CEILING: a high ceiling in which the surface is sloped to follow the roof.

CEILING MEDALLION: a decorative element, often circular and made of plaster, from which a light fixture is suspended; more common in formal rooms.

CENTERLINE: a regulating line used to align the centers of architectural elements.

CHAIR RAIL: a wooden molding placed along the lower part of the wall to prevent chairs, when pushed back, from damaging the wall; also used as decoration; rare in private rooms.

CLAPBOARD: a wood siding commonly used in frame construction, applied horizontally and overlapped, thicker along the lower edge.

COFFERED CEILING: a grid of dropped wooden beams, usually decorative, and recessed panels, often naturally finished and associated with formal rooms.

COLONIAL: in America, Georgian architecture of the 18th century.

COLONNADE: a series of columns supporting an entablature.

COLUMN: an upright structural member consisting of a capital at the top, a long shaft in the middle, and usually a base at the bottom.

COMMODE: a small and decorative cabinet.

COMMON BOND: a pattern of bricks produced when several courses composed entirely of stretchers (the long side of the brick) alternate with one course of headers (the short side).

CONSERVATORY: a room enclosed by glass walls and a glass ceiling.

CORINTHIAN: the third Greek architectural order, characterized by slender proportions and elaborate ornamentation; capitals ornamented with stylized acanthus foliage.

CORNERBOARDS: trim boards on the external corners of frame structures.

CORNICE: a decorative projection along the top of a wall; in classical architecture, the third and uppermost division of an entablature.

COURSE: a row of bricks, blocks, stones, or shingles.

CROWN MOULDING: trim at the top of a wall used to transition to the ceiling; its height and shape varying dramatically, common in formal rooms of styles preceding the 20th century, also used in some private rooms, although of a diminished stature.

D

DADO: in classical architecture the columnar part of a pedestal; an arrangement of paneling and molding around the base of a room resembling a continuous pedestal; a rectangular groove cut across a piece of lumber for receiving another piece.

DENTILS: rectangular blocks spaced closely, used in Ionic, Corinthian, and Composite cornices. In antiquity they emulated wood framing indigenous to the era.

DORIC: the simplest of the classical Greek orders, the preferred style of the Greek mainland (see Parthenon), characterized by sturdy proportions, fluted columns with no base, plain capitals (a circle topped by a square) and a simple but bold entablature.

DORMER: a small roofed structure containing one or more windows, projecting through the sloping roof of a building; originally used for sleeping quarters, hence the name.

DOUBLE-HUNG WINDOW: a window of two offset sashes that slide vertically past each other.

DRAWING ROOM: a room used for the reception or entertainment of guests.

DRY SINK: a sink (usually lined with zinc) with no plumbing, where dishes can be washed.

DUTCH DOOR: an exterior door divided in half horizontally so that the upper and lower halves may be opened or closed independently.

E

EAVE: the lowest edge of a pitched roof; the projecting overhang at the lower edge of a sloping roof.

ELL: an addition or wing to a building perpendicular to its principal dimension, forming an L or a T.

ENGAGED COLUMN: a half or three quarter round column attached to a wall.

ENGLISH BOND: a pattern of bricks produced when courses of stretchers (the long side of the brick) alternate with courses of headers (the short side).

ENTABLATURE: in classical architecture the horizontal component, usually decorated, that lies directly above the columns or pilasters; composed of an architrave, a frieze, and a cornice.

ENTASIS: a slight convex curving of the outline of the shaft of a column so that it is wider in the middle to correct the optical illusion that parallel straight sides appear slightly concave.

ESCUTCHEON: an ornamental or protective metal plate surrounding the door handle or keyhole.

EYEBROW: a low dormer having no sides, the roofing being carried over it in an eyebrow-shaped curve.

F

FACADE: the exterior face of a building usually the front, but any side that is emphasized architecturally.

FARMER'S PORCH: a simple single-story porch with a shed roof supported by modest posts.

FASCIA BOARD: a flat vertical trim piece running horizontally along the eave, used to cover the ends of the rafter tails. Its face is often embellished with a molding, or a gutter.

FEDERAL: a style popular in America after the Revolution; highly symmetrical with a focus on the front entry: a paneled door framed by sidelights and pilasters, often crowned by a fanlight or entablature; a low-pitched roof, sometimes with a balustrade, large windows with double hung sashes having 6 to 12 panes per sash separated by thin muntins.

FIELDSTONE: a stone at the surface of fields, commonly used as a building material.

FIREBOX: the recessed chamber of a fireplace where a fire is maintained.

FLASHING: thin metal sheets or other thin impervious materials installed to prevent moisture infiltration at joints of roof planes and between the roof and the vertical surfaces of roof penetrations or abutting walls.

FLAT SAWN: commonly used to describe a board in which the growth rings intersect the face at an angle between 0 degrees and 45 degrees; also plain sawn.

FLAT STOCK: rectangular trim. If unembellished with a backband usually reserved for private rooms in houses preceding the twentieth century

FLEMISH BOND: a pattern of bricks produced when in each course stretchers (the long side of the brick) alternate with headers (the short side) and the headers of one course are centered above the stretchers of the previous course.

FLUTING: a series of decorative concave vertical grooves cut into the surface of the columns and pilasters of all orders of classical architecture except Tuscan.

FOURSQUARE: (also Prairie Box) a style popular between 1900 and 1930, part of a movement to simple rectilinear architecture; distinguished by its boxlike massing and broad proportions, usually two stories, with a hipped roof, widely overhanging eaves, central dormers, and a one-story porch spanning the facade.

FOYER: the entrance hall or reception hall just inside the main exterior door.

FRENCH COLONIAL: stucco-sided homes with large two-story porches and narrow wooden pillars; originally found in Louisiana and parts of Mississippi.

FRENCH DOOR: usually one of a pair of doors with multiple glass panes extending almost from top to bottom.

FRIEZE: the middle member of an entablature, between the architrave and the cornice, a panel below the upper molding or cornice of a wall; any ornamented horizontal band.

FRONTISPIECE: an elaborate entrance centerpiece, or gate embellishing the center of the main facade.

G

GABLED ROOF: a pitched roof with one downward slope on either side of a central horizontal ridge.

GALVANIC ACTION: a chemical reaction between dissimilar metals in contact in the presence of moisture in which one metal is consumed by corrosion.

GAMBLE HOUSE: designed by Charles Sumner Green and Henry Mather Green for Mary and David Gamble of the Procter and Gamble family; one of the finest examples of Arts-and-Crafts architecture in the world.

GAMBREL ROOF: a pitched roof with two slopes on either side of a central, horizontal ridge, the lower slope having the steeper pitch, giving the look of a traditional American hay barn.

GEORGIAN: the prevailing style of English architecture during the reigns of George I, II, and III (1714–1820), based on the principles of the Italian Renaissance architect Andrea Palladio: spacious, symmetrical, medium-pitch roof, minimal overhang, paired chimneys, paneled front door at center with pilasters, five windows across the front.

GLAZING: the glass used in windows; the process of installing it.

GOLDEN MEAN: a geometric proportion obtained by dividing a line segment unequally such that the shorter line segment is to the larger line segment as the larger is to the whole.

GOTHIC REVIVAL: (1830–1870), initially stone mansions reminiscent of Gothic cathedrals; later and more often, whimsical frame houses with steeply pitched cross gable roofs, bay and oriel windows, windows with pointed arches, a one-story porch, and an asymmetrical floor plan.

GREEK REVIVAL: flourished (1820–1860) in the United States, featured pedimented front gables, symmetry, bold simple moldings, and often a front porch with columns; popular in Southern mansions.

H

HALF-LAPPED JOINT: one board is placed over another and half the thickness of each board is removed for a flush face between boards.

HALF-TIMBERED: in early construction, a wall constructed of timber with the spaces between the timbers filled with masonry or plaster; now used only decoratively.

HEADER: in masonry, a brick or building stone laid across the thickness of the wall with one end, the short side, facing out.

HEARTWOOD: the darker, harder central part of the trunk of a tree, as distinguished from the lighter, softer outer sapwood; usually more resistant to decay.

HIPPED ROOF: a roof with four sloped faces, usually all of the same angle.

HISTORIC: associated with an event or person of significance in history.

HISTORICAL: belonging to a time past.

HUTCH: a cupboard with drawers for storage and usually open shelves or glass doors on top; often used for displaying china.

I

IONIC: an order of classical Greek architecture characterized by slender fluted columns and prominent spirals (volutes) on the capitals.

ITALIANATE: an American architectural style of the mid-19th century, part of a larger Romantic movement in the arts, two or three stories, tall narrow windows, low-pitched roofs with overhanging eaves.

J

JAMB: the side or vertical part of any opening in a wall, such as a door or window.

JOISTS: narrow, tall, and closely spaced wooden framing members that support a floor. These differ from beams, which are larger and used where extra support is needed.

K

KNEE: an angled piece of wood used as a brace.

L

LINTEL: a beam of any material used to span the top of an opening such as that created by a window, door, or fireplace.

LITE: glazing framed by muntins or, when muntins are not present, the sash in a window or door.

LIVING HALL: a room of the Victorian era from which the main stair ascended; sometimes it included a fireplace, and it often served as the formal entry.

LOCKSET: the locking mechanism of a door.

LOFT: a room under the roof of a building; a small area raised in a larger room.

M

MANSARD ROOF: having two slopes on all four sides: an upper slope pitched at the minimum needed to shed water and usually not visible from the ground, a longer almost vertical lower slope with a straight, convex, or concave shape; common to Second Empire houses; originally used in France by Mansart as an architectural trick to reduce the number of stories beneath the eaves and thereby cut taxation.

MASSING: the overall bulk, size, physical volume, or magnitude of a structure.

MERCURY KNOB: a glass door knob with a mirrored face.

MODULE: that dimension of a structure (e.g., the diameter of a column) used as a unit of length by which the rest of the structure is proportioned.

MONITOR: a long structure above and parallel to a roof's ridge, designed to give light and/or ventilation to the interior.

MONOLITHIC: without parts or divisions, as a large stone.

MORTISE: a rectangular hole cut in a board to receive a tenon.

MULLION: a comparatively heavy vertical or horizontal member that separates adjacent windows.

MUNTIN: a slender vertical or horizontal member used to hold and separate panes of glass in a sash or glazed door.

N

NEWEL POST: a principal post in a balustrade, usually larger and more ornate than the balusters, found at the foot of a staircase and at the corners of landings.

NOTRE DAME DE PARIS: a Gothic cathedral in Paris, France; in English usually known simply as Notre Dame; widely considered the finest example of French Gothic architecture.

O

ORDER: a term applied to the styles of classical architecture–Doric, Corinthian, and Ionic of Greece and their Roman derivatives Composite and Tuscan–which specified the proportions and the nature of the constituent parts of columns and entablatures.

P

PALLADIAN WINDOW: a window with three openings, the central one arched and wider than the others, named for Italian Renaissance architect Andrea Palladio, 1508–1580.

PANE: one of the divisions of a window or door, consisting of a single unit of glass set in a frame.

PARLOR: a formal room for family and guests to sit, talk, and relax.

PARQUET FLOOR: a decorative inlaid woodwork, normally in geometric patterns; most common in formal rooms of high style 19th century homes; rare in private rooms.

PARTHENON: called the most perfect Doric temple ever built, the pinnacle of Greek architecture, constructed of marble on the Acropolis in Athens between 447 and 438 B.C.

PEDESTAL: in classical architecture a structure resembling a fat column, placed under a column as its base.

PEDIMENT: the isosceles triangular termination used in classical architecture corresponding to the later gable but more obtuse at the top; includes one horizontal and two raking cornices.

PENDANT LIGHT: a fixture suspended below the ceiling by a stem or chain.

PICTURE RAIL: a molding on the wall near the ceiling to support picture hooks; most common in formal rooms, but sometimes used in bedrooms.

PILASTER: a flat, vertical column engaged with the wall, structural or ornamental, projecting one-third its width or less from a wall.

PITCH: roof slope; measured by the angle of the roof from horizontal.

PLAIN SAWN: commonly used to describe a board in which the growth rings intersect the face at an angle between 0 degrees and 45 degrees; also flat sawn.

PLAN: a diagram of the horizontal organization of space in a building.

PLINTH: a square member forming the lower part of the base of a column or pilaster; also a platform onto which a building is placed for prominence.

POCKET DOOR: a door that slides open into a slot in a wall.

PORTAL: an elongated cased opening used as a transition between rooms of differing formality or to dramatize the height of an adjoining room.

PORTE-COCHERE: a large porch under which vehicles can drive, extending from an entrance over a driveway to shelter those getting in or out of vehicles.

PORTICO: a roofed entrance porch, centerpiece of the facade, with columns like a temple front, often supporting a pediment.

PROPORTION: balance among parts of the whole.

PUTTY GLAZE: a flexible, oil-based material used to affix glass to muntins and sash; historically applied to the outside face of a window and shaped as a bevel around the glass.

Q

QUARTERSAWN: commonly used to describe a board in which the growth rings intersect the face at an angle between 75 degrees and 90 degrees.

QUEEN ANNE: the quintessential American Victorian house with abundant bric-a-brac and gingerbread, an extensive use of wood, elaborate woodwork and an asymmetrical facade; the most popular style from about 1875 until 1900, painted with as many as seven earth tones to bring out the different textures and trim.

R

RABBET: a rectangular notch cut from the edge or face of a board intended to receive another element; for example, the recess into which glazing is installed between muntins in a window sash.

RAFTER: the structural supports of a roof that follow the slope of the roof.

RAFTER TAIL: the exposed end of a rafter seen from the outside, common to 19th century cottages and 20th-century bungalows.

RAIL: a horizontal member of a window sash or paneled door; a bar extending horizontally between supports.

RAKE: a trim board that follows the sloping edge of a gable.

RED OXIDE: a red iron oxide pigment, ferric oxide, with excellent permanence and colorfastness.

REGULATING LINE: a device used in architecture to assist in the placement of building elements.

RIDGE: a horizontal line that is the highest point of certain roofs such as gabled.

RIFT SAWN: commonly used to describe a board in which the growth rings intersect the face at an angle between 45 degrees and 75 degrees.

RIM LOCK: an older style lock mounted to the door face.

ROSETTE: the cylindrical faceplate behind the door knob, affixed to the door face.

RUBBLE STONE: uncut stone.

RUMFORD FIREPLACE: a tall, shallow fireplace known for high thermal efficiency; designed in 1796 by the physicist Benjamin Thompson, later known as Count Rumford; popular from its invention to the 1850s.

RUNNING BOND: a pattern of bricks in which each course is entirely stretchers (the long side of the brick) and the joints of one course are centered above the stretchers of the previous course; also called stretcher bond.

S

SALT BOX: an economical style created when colonists expanded their two-story, gable-roof homes by adding a one-story space at the rear with a shed roof of the same pitch and width as the original roof, producing a shape like a Colonial-era salt container.

SASH: the framework of a window, movable or fixed, in which the panes of glass are set; may slide vertically as in a double-hung window or pivot as in a casement window.

SASH LOCK: a finger operated device used to preclude the movement of either or both sashes of a window.

SCARF: a joint made by cutting two pieces so that they overlap firmly, forming one continuous piece.

SCONCE: a wall-mounted light fixture.

SETBACK: in zoning ordinances, that distance from the property lines beyond which one may not build.

SHAFT: in classical columns, the cylindrical part between the base and the capital, normally fluted, tapered (the top being 85 percent the diameter of the bottom) to appear taller, and swollen very slightly toward the middle (entasis) so that the maximum diameter occurs about one-third the way up.

SHED DORMER: having a single sloped roof; most economical dormer shape and common on facades out of public view.

SHED ROOF: a roof having one sloping plane.

SHINGLE STYLE: developed by H. H. Richardson (1836–1886) and McKim, Mead & White in Boston around 1880; favored for the seaside estates of the New England coast, borrows wide porches, shingled surfaces, and asymmetrical forms from Queen Anne style; normally two or three stories tall, on a heavy stone foundation, with qualities of weight, density, and permanence pronounced; asymmetrical; shingles form a continuous covering, stretched smooth over roof lines and around corners; large rooms and porches loosely arranged around an open great hall dominated by a grand staircase.

SHIPLAP: in residential construction a wood plank from 3 to 10 in. wide and ¾ in. thick with ⅜ in. rabbets on both edges so that a watertight seal and a smooth surface result when it is installed horizontally as a siding.

SIDELIGHT: an area of fixed glass alongside a door or window.

SILL: the horizontal bottom member of a window or door frame.

SOFFIT: the underside of any overhead architectural element, such as an arch, architrave, balcony, beam, cornice, eave, or lintel. Most commonly refers to the underside of a roof eave.

SPANISH COLONIAL: most commonly in the Southwest, Florida, and California, based on Hispanic and Moorish traditions, sided in adobe or stucco, flat or slightly pitched roofs finished with red clay tiles, sometimes with a second-story porch.

STILE: the vertical side structural members of a window sash or paneled door.

STORM PANEL: an extra layer of glazing installed to limit heat loss through a window or door.

STRETCHER: in masonry, a brick or stone laid horizontally with its length in the direction of the face of the wall, i.e., with the long side facing out.

STUCCO: a plaster or cement used as a wall coating; especially a fine plaster composed of lime or gypsum with sand and powdered marble.

SURROUND: that which surrounds, such as the trim, tile, or glazing around a door, a fireplace, or a window.

SWAG: in classical architecture a garland of flowers, foliage, fruit, or ribbons suspended in a curve between two rosettes, used as decoration.

T

TENON: a rectangular projection on the end of a piece of wood for insertion into a socket or mortise.

THERMAL PANE: usually two sheets of glass hermetically sealed together at the edges, entrapping an insulating layer of gas between them.

THUMB LATCH: a door latch operated by placing the thumb on a lever that raises the latch.

TRANSOM LIGHT: a light above the transom bar of a door.

TRAY CEILING: a ceiling resembling an inverted serving tray, sloping near the edge of the room, usually to accommodate the roof.

TUDOR REVIVAL: derived primarily from English Renaissance buildings of the 16th and early 17th centuries, popular in the suburbs from 1920 to 1940, feature overlapping gables, slate roofs, half-timbering.

TURNED GABLE: a gable roof in which the ridge is turned 90 degrees to the main roof, exposing the triangular end wall or gable portion of the roof.

V

VANITY: historically a dressing table; today, a cabinet supporting a sink in a bathroom.

VARIANCE: a permit for construction that does not to conform to specific zoning ordinances.

VENEER PLASTER: a thin layer of plaster laid over water-proofed gypsum board.

VERANDA: an open porch or portico extending along the perimeter of a building.

VERGEBOARD: a board, often ornate, attached to the pair of outside rafters forming the projection of a gabled roof, especially in Tudor or Gothic architecture; also known as a bargeboard.

VESTIBULE: a small room at the entrance, an ante-room.

VICTORIAN STYLE: usually includes the Stick, Queen Anne, and Shingle styles popular during Queen Victoria's reign (1840–1901), but excludes the Romantic Revivals.

VOLUTE: in classical architecture, the scroll-like spiral ornament on Ionic, Corinthian, and Composite capitals. A common shape given to the terminus of a handrail in the Federal and Greek Revival periods.

W

WAINSCOTING: decorative wood paneling on an interior wall, now usually the lower three or four ft.; in Colonial America, the entire wall.